A Call to Service

A Call to Service

JOHN KERRY

[Viking]

VIKING
Published by the Penguin Group
Penguin Group (USA) Inc., 375 Hudson Street,
New York, New York 10014, U.S.A.
Penguin Books Ltd, 80 Strand,
London WC2R 0RL, England
Penguin Books Australia Ltd, 250 Camberwell Road, Camberwell,
Victoria 3124, Australia
Penguin Books Canada Ltd, 10 Alcorn Avenue,
Toronto, Ontario, Canada M4V 3B2
Penguin Books India (P) Ltd, 11 Community Centre, Panchsheel Park,
New Dehli - 110 017, India
Penguin Books (N. Z.) Ltd, Cnr Rosedale and Airborne Roads, Albany,
Auckland, New Zealand
Penguin Books (South Africa) (Pty) Ltd, 24 Sturdee Avenue,
Rosebank, Johannesburg 2196, South Africa

Penguin Books Ltd, Registered Offices:
80 Strand, London WC2R 0RL, England

First published in 2003 by Viking Penguin,
a member of Penguin Group (USA) Inc.

1   3   5   7   9   10   8   6   4   2

CIP data available

ISBN 0-670-03260-3

This book is printed on acid-free paper. ∞

Printed in the United States of America

To my mother, my father, and the future

Contents

★

Preface

★

Twelve years ago, late one night, I found myself on a C-135 transport plane that was taking me and two senatorial colleagues on the long flight across Europe and the Middle East to Kuwait. The Persian Gulf War had only recently ended, and we were headed for a postwar inspection tour of the region.

John Glenn, John McCain, and I had been discussing our shared love of flying until John Glenn fell asleep. And now John McCain and I sat in uncomfortable silence for a few moments until, inevitably, we started talking not about the Gulf War but about *our* war—Vietnam.

Though we had served together in the U.S. Senate for nearly five years at that point, we had never yet shared our common and separate experiences in Vietnam. We were aware of each other's public stories, of course. I knew that John—the son of a distinguished admiral—had been a

Navy pilot who was shot down over North Vietnam, where he was held, beaten, and tortured for five and a half years, much of that time served after he refused to accept freedom on terms that violated the POW code of honor governing the order of prisoner releases.

And John knew I had also been a Navy officer, commanding a "swift boat"—a small, fast patrol boat used for counterinsurgency missions—in the Mekong Delta for two tours of duty. Unlike him, I had been able to come back after I received my third Purple Heart. Upon my return, however, based on my strong feelings that our fighting men were being sacrificed for a mission in which our leaders no longer believed, I got involved in the effort of veterans to stop the war.

Not surprisingly John, who was still imprisoned in the Hanoi Hilton at that time, took a dim view of my antiwar activities and, in fact, campaigned for my Republican opponent when I first ran for the U.S. Senate in 1984. But he didn't really know the story of my personal experiences in Vietnam, just as I didn't really know his.

The gulf between us on that issue was typical. In those difficult years of the Vietnam War there were too many on both the left and right in this country, along with the Communists in Vietnam, who had tried to pit those who had worn the uniform and now opposed the war against those who still supported it and who, whether on the battlefields or in prison cells in Hanoi, continued to serve with the greatest of valor. John McCain and I were caught up in that crossfire, started by those who wanted differences over the war to become fundamental differences between two soldiers.

I don't know exactly how long we talked about Vietnam in that dark C-135 cabin, but by daybreak we shared a new understanding—and a new friendship. And we built upon that friendship over the next few years to bring our war, finally, to an end.

Later that year, I was asked by the Senate majority leader to chair a special committee on POW/MIA affairs, in part because of continuing media reports—and family hopes that they raised—that a significant number of Americans were still being secretly held in Vietnam. This issue, moreover, had led to the continuation of our economic boycott against Vietnam and our refusal to resume normal diplomatic relations with that country even though the hostilities had ended nearly two decades earlier. John McCain also agreed to serve on this committee.

Both of us had signed up for what was generally regarded as one of the most thankless tasks in Washington. We had to review a thousand old documents, struggle to achieve some level of cooperation from a Vietnamese government that had hundreds of thousands of its own MIAs, and deal with a POW/MIA advocacy network that fed every wild rumor or conspiracy theory, preying on the grief of families of Americans who had not come home. We had to fight against the Rambo psychology of reopening all the contentious issues of the war all over again, and—for John McCain and me, at any rate—we had to come to grips with our own memories.

I certainly remembered how close I had come to being killed by rifle fire and rocket launchers from the shore in our forays deep into Viet Cong territory. I remembered crew members and close friends who didn't come back. I knew I could have wound up, like John McCain and the sons and husbands of those who anxiously followed our hearings, a POW or MIA.

We made a total of eight trips to Vietnam during and immediately after our hearings. These visits were filled with unforgettable experiences, and one of the most deeply moving of them was accompanying John to the site of the Hanoi Hilton and seeing the tiny room—really almost a cage—where he sacrificed a good part of his young adulthood for his country, in pain and fear and isolation.

I have had no greater privilege in all my life than finding, then standing on, common ground with John McCain, with whom I formed a close personal and political alliance during these hearings. We insisted on examining all the evidence, demanded that witnesses be held accountable for the reliability of their testimony, and, in the end, convinced the entire committee to agree on a report that concluded that there were likely no Americans still alive in Vietnam.

And our alliance continued to the next steps our country needed to take to honorably put the war behind us—abandonment of the economic boycott against Vietnam and normalization of diplomatic relations. President Clinton had the courage to put these policies into action, and he still says that he couldn't have done it without the constant presence and united support of two Vietnam vets named John—one a Democrat, one a Republican; one a famous POW, the other a famous war protester. As for me, I'm most proud of the fact that when we say the word "Vietnam" today we mean not just a war but a country—at long last, a place where, as I hoped thirty years ago, "America turned and veterans helped in the turning."

My friendship with John McCain has continued and even strengthened after our last Vietnam mission, and neither of us has much use for those in either party who complain that we should keep to our own partisan interests. In fact, we have discovered that we share something far more precious than party: a common call to service.

I learned several important lessons during our effort to put the war behind us for ourselves, our generation, and our country.

I learned how to reach across partisan and ideological divides to find common ground in the rich soil of American values and experiences.

I learned how to overcome the passionate convictions of narrow interest groups to build a consensus based on facts rather than prejudice.

I learned how to make my personal experiences a platform for broader lessons about American ideals and their special place in the world's struggle for peace and justice.

And perhaps most important, I learned that the call to service did not end with a discharge from the Navy or election to the United States Senate.

I'm pretty sure that our mutual experience in transcending the Vietnam trauma was one important factor that led John McCain to run for president in 2000 as a serious reformer, a "straight talker," and a patriot who believes our willingness to meet domestic challenges is as important a test of national will as our willingness to engage in warfare. He did his best to summon his party to rise to such values, and had he succeeded, the country would be in much better hands today.

I don't believe there's much left in the Republican Party of the spirit of true civic service or the courage to defy powerful interests and seriously address the most pressing national issues. And too many people in my own Democratic Party are focused on narrow interests and as a result have too little vision of the vast potential for achievement, at home and abroad, for the United States under the kind of leadership we deserve.

It's time for a new call to service. It's time to rally Democrats, Republicans, and independents alike to face the common challenges of this generation. In the course of my career, from the Mekong Delta to the Senate, I've tried to muster the right combination of the toughness to govern and the compassion to care—along with a deep commitment to justice and to America's progressive values. But my experiences have taught me that a leader succeeds only to the extent that he is able to communicate his values, his goals, his ideas, and much of who he is in direct communication, one on one. I began that kind of conversation with

John McCain on a C-135 late one night, and it's continued ever since. I want to begin that conversation with my fellow citizens in this book and during this presidential campaign, and continue it while we work together to meet the challenges of our age.

A Call to Service

Why I Am Running
for President

★

I am a child of the greatest generation of Americans and therefore a member of the most fortunate generation of Americans. Like my parents, I have always hoped and often assumed that my own children will have more opportunities in life than I had and will live in a country and in a world where such opportunities are more widely shared and more deeply rooted than at any time in the past.

I am running for president in no small part to redeem that promise for the America to come. While we are living today in the most extraordinary and powerful nation on earth, I believe not only that America's best days are still to come but that our best work is yet to be done. We have the capacity to lift the life of our own land as well as lead the world to a safer and more hopeful future. But doing so will require equal measures of strength, vision, and resolve, embodied in a leadership that grasps both the breadth of our potential and the great legacy of our past.

As Americans, we inherit with our birthright of free-dom a sacred chain of responsibility that stretches back to the Founders and to the sacrifices of the immigrants who built this country before and after them and extends to the present day. Our task is not just to guarantee material progress: along with a better life we must pass on to our children that unique sense of optimism and that God-given belief in the universal appeal of our ideals that have always marked our national character.

I look ahead with confidence, because all around us I see evidence that the children of the baby-boom gener-ation have the right stuff. The skill and courage of the young men and women who went into harm's way in Afghanistan and Iraq—and for that matter, at ground zero in New York—match the best of my generation during the cold war and my parents' generation during the Second World War.

In that conflict my father flew DC-3s in the Army Air Corps. Afterward, he entered the diplomatic service and was privileged to be an active participant during the his-toric period when this nation forged a "grand and global al-liance" against tyranny with measures that ranged from the Marshall Plan through NATO to a host of multilateral in-stitutions. His was the greatest generation not just because it defeated Fascism but because it was determined after the war to create a nation worthy of all the effort and sacrifice that had been made and a world worthy of the cause for which they had fought.

My parents raised me with a belief in patriotism and

service. After I joined the Navy during the Vietnam War, I commanded a naval gunboat patrolling the Mekong Delta. Then when I came home after two tours of duty, I decided that the same sense of service demanded something more of me. This led me to protest the very war in which I had fought, while always honoring those who fought before me, with me, and after me.

It may be hard to understand three decades later, but for all the conflict and contention over Vietnam here at home, this period was also a time when the people of our country were drawn into a great civic discourse. Critical national issues had come to the center of people's everyday lives. We had both the burden and the honor of facing in a short span of time a long list of topics that would fundamentally change our lives—civil rights, women's rights, the environment, economic opportunity, and reclaiming democracy itself from elected leaders who lied to us and broke the laws they were sworn to uphold. We Americans took our country back and moved our country forward. That was the real America for which I had fought in the Vietnam War and in the antiwar movement, and I am still convinced—and can cite witnesses across the former Soviet empire who will confirm my belief—that it was the power of our values as much as the power of weapons that finally won the cold war.

In world war and in cold war, our people never lost the determination to make sure that our country was truly the best it could be. They knew there were things worth fighting for, both at home and abroad. It is that determination I hope to bring to the election of 2004, to the presidency of the United States, and to the common challenges Americans face.

*

There's a famous old saying that all leaders tend to be either hedgehogs or foxes. A hedgehog knows one thing very well, and a fox knows a little about everything. I suspect I would qualify as a hedgehog who's been around the field a few times. In the course of my public career, I've had the chance to master a range of issues—veterans issues after the war, crime as a prosecutor, economic development as a lieutenant governor, and then foreign policy, health care, intelligence, national defense, drug trafficking, technology, and education during nineteen years as a U.S. senator.

I don't consider myself a policy wonk, but I was brought up to care about the big issues and to think for myself, not hire others to do the thinking for me.

While my father, Richard Kerry, was serving as a diplomat, my mother, Rosemary, became a serious civic activist and an environmentalist before the word "ecology" was widely used. And I first got to know my wife, Teresa, at a policy conference in South America. It's no surprise that I'm accustomed to talking about ideas and world events around the dinner table and that my family is a central part of my political life. We've kept up the tradition with my daughters, Alex and Vanessa, and my stepsons, John, Andre, and Chris. They've all been nurtured on a steady diet of civic obligation.

I've also benefited from a pretty remarkable extended family of people who have influenced my thinking and helped keep me humble and hungry for knowledge.

First and foremost have been my brothers-in-arms from Vietnam, my crewmates from PCF 94 and PCF 44. We came from different states and backgrounds, but all that really mattered was that we were all from America. My real growing up came with them on a fragile boat under enemy fire halfway across the world. Thirty-five years later, they still help me keep my bearings. We share a precious, unshakable bond that veterans understand and others respect.

While I was an antiwar activist and veterans advocate after Vietnam, my extended family grew to include thousands who had always passionately loved their country and often passionately disagreed with one another about how to fight for their country's values. After I testified before the Senate Foreign Relations Committee on behalf of the Vietnam Veterans Against the War, I felt as if I had heard from every one of them, whether happy, angry, approving, or damning, along with their parents, their wives and girlfriends, and their children. And I quickly learned to listen to the veterans of World War II and Korea who shared our sacrifices but didn't like our long hair, our music, or our challenges to authority.

All these experiences helped me deal with the ultimate extended family of constituents I have represented in elected office. I will never forget meeting crime victims as an assistant district attorney in Middlesex County, Massachusetts. Crime too often is reduced to a statistic, but from each of them, I learned that every act of violence gives rise to an individual human tragedy. Since then, as lieutenant governor and as a senator, I've talked with countless citizens, often in happy moments but often, too, at some of the hard-

est times in their lives—men and women displaced from their homes by natural disasters or from their jobs by technological change; families overwhelmed by health-care costs or frustrated by bad schools; citizens struggling to obtain medical benefits for their parents or get questions answered by bureaucrats. I can't say I've heard it all, but I have heard a lot, and I've tried to learn something from every encounter with a person, a problem, or an idea that crosses my path.

I don't think it's an exaggeration at all to say that the 2004 election represents a real crossroads for our country.

During the 1990s we were actually beginning to make real progress on a range of national problems that people had pretty much come to regard as immutable parts of the landscape. Violent crime fell sharply after nearly twenty-five years of steady increases. Welfare dependency was down by more than half. Teen pregnancy and abortion rates decreased. We adopted tough measures to reduce acid rain and raise water quality. Inner cities were being reborn all across the country. Real incomes rose for the middle class for the first time in two decades. Health-care costs stabilized. Technological innovations exploded, and productivity increased dramatically. Millions of working families—for the first time ever, a majority in this nation or any nation—joined the investor class, and America created the first mass upper-middle class in human history. Nearly thirty years of federal budget deficits were replaced by budget surpluses so large as to defy the imagination. From a statistical point of view, nearly everything good went up and nearly everything bad went down. And all this progress occurred despite partisan warfare and gridlock in Congress, and an administration under Bill Clinton that became more and more distracted and embattled by endless allegations and the investigations that grew out of them.

While we can't go back to the exact policies of the Clinton years—as a progressive, I believe we should always be looking forward and embracing change—it is hard to believe that most people wouldn't want to go back to the kind of results they helped achieve. Instead, in the name of ideology and on behalf of selfish interests, the Bush administration has been systematically dismantling just about everything government accomplished during the 1990s: environmental protection, international diplomacy, substantial investments in basic scientific and technological research, fiscal discipline, and the commitment to a fairer society of opportunity for all. Not surprisingly, its policies have begun to have seriously alarming consequences: a sluggish economy, rising crime, the largest budget deficits in history, and the weakening of our alliances and standing around the world. Another four years of the Bush agenda, especially if there is a Republican Congress, will take this country so far off track that it could take a generation to put things right again.

But if we put the country back on a progressive course in 2004, I believe we can rebuild the prosperity of the 1990s, reverse a long series of bad decisions and evasions of responsibility, restore America's world leadership in the eyes of our friends and our enemies alike, and protect the liberties that make this country a beacon to the hopeful and a reproach to tyrants everywhere. We have the chance to truly protect Americans from terrorism at home and abroad while calling on all Americans to join in the fulfillment of our freedom and democracy.

The time has come to renew our best hopes, take up the great unfinished business of our society, and take on the big challenges that many people have come to consider as hopeless, challenges like achieving energy independence, providing universal access to health care, creating high-quality schools for all students, using technology to drastically reform how government works, and turning the rhetoric of worker-controlled lifelong learning into a reality. And if I have anything to say about it, we will also make a commitment to political and civic reform, turning the tide of cynicism and indifference about politics and government and making our democracy both far more participatory and truly representative.

My fellow Democrats don't agree on all of these issues or how exactly to resolve them, and that's as it should be. I want my party to be an open door for lively debate, not a mirror image of the narrow ideological sect that the Republicans are becoming. Most of us, however, do agree that George W. Bush is leading America in a very dangerous direction. While we all admired the way he rallied the nation after 9/11, we also believe that he is, by ideology, inclination, and experience, incapable of keeping America strong enough at home or abroad to sustain us in peace or in war over the long haul. The question we now face is how to make that case to the widest span of the American people—Democrats, independents, and moderate Republicans alike—and offer a clear alternative agenda.

I, like so many of my fellow Democrats, am still angry about the painful and protracted events that followed the 2000 election and that perhaps altered its outcome. We should channel this anger into positive grassroots energy and into a determination never to let voters be disenfranchised again.

President Bush has enough bad policies on which to focus our energies; there is no need to ascribe to him a weak intellect or bad intentions as a political strategy. We should not deny him his few successes or refuse to acknowledge the affection his plainspokenness and quiet self-confidence inspire in many. For my part, I intend to run a presidential campaign organized around a contest of ideas, values, and policies, rather than a clash of personalities or a war between political tribes.

To those who think that sounds naïve, I would point to my last contested senatorial reelection campaign, in 1996, when I was challenged by William Weld, a very popular incumbent governor. There's no question that that campaign could have degenerated into a mud bath if we had let it. It was a close race between two longtime statewide elected officials with nearly universal name recognition, the kind of race that is often decided by turnout. We both had advisers who urged us to focus on "energizing" our supporters with emotional appeals and attack ads and forget about persuading the relatively small group of undecided voters. But Governor Weld and I chose another path for our campaigns—a long series of debates rigorously focused on issues rather than personalities, a process that let voters reach their own judgments about our differences, our characters, and our capacity for leadership. By the end of that campaign, we all sincerely felt we were part of something unique and valuable, which had not only raised the level of civic discourse in Massachusetts but had actually boosted voter turnout through positive rather than negative means.

That's precisely the kind of contest I would like to have with George W. Bush, and it's one that I believe will serve the nation well.

President Bill Clinton once said that running for the presidency against an incumbent is like an extended job interview with the American people: You have to convince voters to fire the chief executive, then hire you as the replacement. I would add to that sentiment that you don't have any business running for the presidency if you don't know and can't explain exactly how you would do a better job.

My case for sending George W. Bush back to his ranch in Crawford, Texas, is based on three big promises he made when he was in my position in the year 2000, then subsequently abandoned.

First, he pledged over and over again to "change the tone" in Washington—to reach out to Democrats and all Americans and overcome the partisan bitterness of the late 1990s. That promise became much more important when he took office after having lost the popular vote, becoming president only by virtue of an eternally controversial ruling by the narrowest possible majority of the U.S. Supreme Court. But since then the president has done the very opposite of what he promised, presiding over the most partisan administration I have experienced in my nearly twenty years in the Senate. He reaches out to Democrats only occasionally, primarily to invite surrender to his political and legislative demands. The tone in Washington, despite the longing for unity inspired by 9/11, is so poisonously partisan that a growing majority of Americans—who have become either nonvoters or independents—are no longer allied with either side. The president and his closest colleagues have personally contributed to this toxic atmosphere by denouncing any thoughtful differences of opinion as unpatriotic, cynically invoking loyalty in the service of party obedience.

Second, George W. Bush pledged frequently to temper the harsh ideology of his party with a "compassionate conservatism" that would harness our nation's civic energy in the pursuit of justice and opportunity for the poor and forgotten. There is no question that the president has broken this promise as well. His one exercise in compassion was the No Child Left Behind Act of 2001, an education reform effort that I supported. The stated purpose of that legislation was to offer a new bargain to states and school districts, under which they would accept greater accountability for results in exchange for the resources and the flexibility to get the job done. The Bush administration began welshing on its side of the bargain almost before the ink was dry on the bill, undermining education funding as part of a larger strategy of directing every available dollar toward tax cuts for the wealthiest Americans. This has been sadly typical of the administration's approach to government: a rhetoric of compassion and concern accompanied by policies that are compassionate primarily toward the most comfortable members of our society.

And that leads me to the third big promise the president has broken. He pledged many times to usher in a "responsibility era," to exercise brave leadership whatever the political costs, and, in the words he used in the 2003 State of the Union Address, not to "pass along our problems to other Congresses, other presidents, and other generations." By reneging on this promise the president has betrayed his claim to represent the mature and responsible face of the baby-boom generation. Among the many dangers the administration is refusing to deal with are global climate change, the impending crisis in retirement programs, the culture of corporate corruption, the need for a genuine homeland security system, our vulnerability to energy blackmail, the "loose nukes" problem in the former Soviet Union, and the threat of worldwide economic deflation. This is the first administration since Calvin Coolidge's that believes that the national government can't do anything about the economy other than giving more to those who already have the most. And this is the same administration that has managed to pass along trillions of dollars in new debt, along with neglect of big national challenges, to future generations.

In my campaign I intend to hold the president accountable for breaking all three of his big promises, applying the very standards he set for himself. And there's an even more fundamental issue upon which I intend to pose the choice between another term for George W. Bush and a Kerry administration. It is a question central to all the challenges our country faces in the new world created by the end of the cold war with communism and the beginning of a war with terrorist networks and other globalized threats to our security. I believe what America needs is a president determined to restore our sense of *common national purpose.*

No matter what issue, foreign or domestic, I address—no matter where in the country I'm speaking, no matter the audience—my underlying message will be the same: *It's time to renew a sense of common purpose.* It is a quality our nation has been losing for several decades—indeed, for much of my lifetime—and it is a quality I firmly believe we must restore. My presidential campaign will be built around the ideas of shared endeavor, national service, intergenerational obligation, and activism aimed at overcoming partisan and personal rivalries to meet the demands of a decisive, even fateful, era. That's why I've titled this book *A Call to Service.* I hear that call, and I believe most Americans are ready to hear it as well and to respond to it. But it's not a call they will hear from George W. Bush, who in the days after 9/11 so memorably asked Americans to shop and travel as their contribution to the fight against terrorism.

From that moment on there's been a striking contrast between the president's willingness to use stirring patriotic rhetoric and his unwillingness to apply the true spirit of patriotism to any aspect of national policy beyond actual military operations. As only one example, he broke a promise in the 2002 State of the Union Address to provide more opportunities for national service by passively accepting congressional Republican efforts to gut the AmeriCorps program that offers precisely such opportunities.

There are literally hundreds of issues on which I strongly disagree with the Bush administration and a Republicanism that's drifted far from its roots as the party of Lincoln and is obsessed with dividing the Union that Lincoln saved. The one policy that bothers me most is their deliberate and consistent effort to undermine the ideal of shared sacrifice and purpose, devotion to the common good, and responsibility to future generations.

Instead this administration has made its top wartime priority the easing of the tax burden on its wealthiest citizens—the citizens least likely to face sacrifices at home or abroad in a time of war. This president has all but endorsed the most invidious conservative policy of our time: that cutting taxes for the people who least need help, turning budget surpluses into deficits, and piling debts on our children are all useful strategies because they will effectively paralyze our own government—the instrument of our democracy—by denying it the revenues to pay for progress. Using tax dollars paid by all Americans to comfort the comfortable while starving the commonwealth has become an item of orthodoxy for a Republican Party that has left behind not only millions of children, not only its promises, but its own honorable traditions of moderation and national stewardship.

Whether it's an energy policy that perpetuates dependence on Middle Eastern oil, an environmental policy that denies global climate change, a health-care policy that proposes to dismantle Medicare and Medicaid, a civil rights policy that pretends to be color-blind while denying educational opportunity to all Americans, or a judicial philosophy that would appoint activist judges determined to validate discrimination or repudiate a woman's right to choose, this is not an administration focused on our long-term interests as a nation. This is an administration that is exploiting our national security challenges as a rationale for dismantling the achievements of a progressive era that lasted from Theodore Roosevelt to Bill Clinton, and taking America back to a system of go-it-alone economics and politics.

This dismantling of the commonwealth is fundamentally corrosive of our national strength, not just at home but ultimately abroad as well. I believe Americans sense that we can and must do better, and my aim is to mobilize a new national resolve to rebuild our commonwealth and with it our strength. I believe America's destiny is to become a living testament to what free human beings can accomplish by acting in unity. The administration currently in the White House apparently believes we can't accomplish anything together other than waging war. That's the contrast I will constantly draw during this campaign, and it's one that will give Americans a clear, even stark, choice in November of 2004.

★

Every successful political message conveys three things: values and goals, then ideas or proposals to reach those goals. To put it another way, all candidates must explain who they are, what they want to do, and how they want to do it.

We Democrats have traditionally been very good at that last step—talking about our programs. We sometimes forget, however, to explain just what our programs are supposed to accomplish. And far too many of us are likewise uncomfortable talking about our own values.

But a presidential contest is an arena in which you inevitably reveal who you are and what you're made of just in the course of dealing with the pressures of the campaign itself. Some candidates fall apart or self-destruct over the very subject of how they define themselves as people. It's crucial to be true to yourself and true to your record of thoughts, words, and deeds, recognizing at the same time that the world changes and that how you apply your values must evolve like life itself.

Some political insiders have called me aloof over the years. I have a feeling that my spending not one weekend in Washington for more than seventeen years may have something to do with that label. I'm not aloof at all with the colleagues, friends, and constituents I have spent time with when I'm away from Washington.

Likewise, I've been misunderstood for having come from a comfortable background. That is certainly true, but it was a background built on a foundation of duty and service, which my family considered a responsibility. And I am deeply grateful to have served

America, to have done my part, no matter how small, to help our great nation.

Fortunately, I recognize that life is more than politics or power.

As someone might guess from my early decision to serve on fast boats in the Navy, I love pastimes that bring together the sky, wind, and surf. One of my favorite sports, in fact, is windsurfing, followed by sailing as a close second. I'm a trained glider pilot but generally fly with an engine. In the winter, I love to ski and skate, and I am so addicted to ice hockey that I still fantasize about starting a professional over-fifty senior league.

I have been an avid biker (bicycle and motorcycle) all my life. I bought a Harley-Davidson last year and have been trying to talk Teresa into riding with me ever since. I rarely get time to ride now, which I'm confident pleases her greatly. If there was an ESPN 1½, I would be a charter subscriber.

But all this is just background music to the main theme of my life right now. I don't want the Democrats to nominate me because I'm a charter member of one of the most selective but fastest growing sports clubs in the world: the NASCAR fans of Massachusetts. I don't intend to challenge President Bush to a contest of who's a more regular guy. I will, however, challenge him to a contest of ideas and vision, and I'm confident I will be able to compete from a position of strength.

★

Beating an incumbent president is always a difficult task. Doing so in a period of external threat to the nation is even harder. Moreover, this administration can call on almost unlimited campaign money and a fanatically loyal right-wing party base that looks forward to a second Bush term as the pot of gold at the end of a rainbow they've been chasing for decades. Finally, the Bush administration is among the most bellicose in our history, determined to have a second term in the White House.

To win this election in the face of such opposition we're going to have to be especially self-disciplined, focused, and loyal to the broad interests of the nation. We can't afford a self-indulgent campaign that congratulates us for our superior virtue as Democrats while alienating a majority of the voting public. We can't treat the Bush administration's errors and faults as self-evident; we will have to explain them in specific detail every day to voters who are as skeptical of us as they are of the Republicans. We aren't going to win merely by energizing ourselves and getting a big Democratic turnout, although we can't win without doing that. With about one-third of the electorate unattached to either party and with at least one-third of voting-age citizens not even bothering to vote, we must make this a campaign of persuasion as well as mobilization.

Republicans will obviously have their own version of what distinguishes the two parties, arguing that we are addicted to government programs, alienated from mainstream values, and unwilling to use the best military in the world to defend the American people in a time of war. We must never accept these stereotypes. I will say all across this country that patriotism and the flag don't belong to any president or any party but to all Americans. And if I am the Democratic nominee, I will proudly proclaim the values that make us Democrats: our commitment to equal opportunity; our belief that economic growth is built on the work and talent of all our people; our commitment to international rules and institutions that promote peace, security, prosperity, freedom and democracy; our concern for a vibrant and participatory democracy here at home; our willingness to meet national challenges before they become emergencies; and, above all, our determination to make government not an end in itself but a vehicle for the achievement of common goals.

I argued in 2002 that Democrats were making a big mistake by dealing with every defense and foreign policy issue by supporting the president and changing the subject, opposing the president and changing the subject, or simply changing the subject from the get-go. They tried instead to address the insecurity of the American people by just offering them prescription drug coverage, but the tactic didn't work. And I'm not ashamed to say it shouldn't have worked. A national political party with nothing much to say about national security in a time of war is evading its responsibilities.

In contrast to the dangerous mix of isolationism and unilateralism that characterizes the Republicans, my kind of Democrat should speak from a position of strength on international issues. That position is the tough-minded, multilateral cooperative tradition of democratic internationalism forged by Woodrow Wilson and Franklin D. Roosevelt in the course of two world wars and by Harry Truman and John F. Kennedy in the cold war. It acknowledges that multilateral organizations—all created at the initiative of the United States—are vehicles for the promotion of our ideals and the protection of our interests around the world. And it recognizes that those ideals and interests in this globalized world are consistent with the peace, prosperity, and self-determination of every country on earth.

Democratic internationalists understand that there are times when America must challenge the UN, NATO, and our allies to stand up for their own preferred values. And they also realize that there are times when America must be challenged to live up to its values as well. That is why I view my own service in the Navy in the Vietnam War and my public dissent from the direction of that war before and after I served as two sides of the same coin. America has taken a rare step in human history in arguing that its interests and the world's are one. I fully accept the challenge of moral as well as military leadership that that claim demands.

Beyond national security issues, I will urge Democrats and Republicans alike to get out of the habit of thinking of issues as belonging exclusively to one party or another. After Democrats made that mistake in the 1970s and 1980s, Bill Clinton was elected and reelected president in no small part because he refused to play this game of issue ownership. Instead of treating national defense, crime, welfare reform, fiscal discipline, or economic development as enemy

territory to be avoided at all costs, he came up with progressive positions on these issues, which not only changed
the perception that Democrats didn't care about them but
also challenged Republicans to come up with proposals on
"Democratic issues," like health care and education.

As President Clinton understood, the people who actually cast votes do not have brains divided into left and
right ideological segments that vibrate only when stimu-
lated by particular liberal or conservative messages. Americans expect their elected officials to have a constructive
solution to every national problem. More to the point,
Democrats cannot truly hold President Bush responsible for
the vast, phony Potemkin Village of his nice-sounding but
empty domestic policies unless we hold ourselves responsible for articulating our policies on "their" defense and foreign policy issues. If I'm leading the Democratic Party in
2004, I will present a 360-degree view of where America is
today, and I will articulate it in a language that speaks to
everyone instead of just preaching to the choir.

Another part of the Democratic heritage that I want to
reclaim is the ability to appeal to Americans as Americans.

Though it's one of our oldest traditions to stand for
equal opportunity for all and special privileges for none, we
Democrats have gotten out of the habit of appealing to
voters as citizens of the United States and have instead
sometimes addressed them primarily as members of interest
or constituency groups or as consumers of government
benefits and tax cuts.

To be sure, millions of Americans belong to groups of

people who have been marginalized in today's politics or, worse yet, have not yet achieved full political rights. One of the core values of the Democratic Party, past, present, and future, is to include the excluded and champion the disenfranchised. Our goal should be to offer every American the chance to transcend group differences, and our goal for America should be to make those things we have in common more important than those things that divide us. We must show that Democrats take unity and diversity—issues that have been given only token attention by Republicans—seriously.

The best place to start this process is by making it clear that Democrats will not contract out our commitment to equal opportunity to any organization that claims to speak for groups of American citizens. For my part, I will not have a subdivided campaign message or campaign structure that's different for men or women, African Americans or Hispanics, gays and lesbians or heterosexuals, Catholics, Protestants, and Jews or the irreligious—or any other way we can segment the electorate. Every single person in my campaign will be attentive not just to Democrats whose rights have been disrespected in the past but to any citizens in the same position. In my view, civil rights are as important to the majority as to any minority, and we must all stand or fall together on our commitment to full, unconditional, affirmative, and assertive equal opportunity for every American.

It's precisely our willingness to demand the aggressive

pursuit of equal opportunity as a basic part of the American creed that distinguishes Democrats from Republicans. We're not a coalition of groups demanding programs or power; we're a coalition of American citizens asking for the same rights for and obligations of one another.

As fate would have it, I learned a new personal lesson about diversity and the American mosaic late last year. Anticipating my candidacy, the Boston Globe *looked into my family history. Among other things, the paper discovered that one hundred years ago, my paternal grandfather was an Austrian Jew named Fritz Kohn, who changed his name to Kerry and converted to Catholicism shortly before immigrating to Massachusetts. I didn't know this because my grandfather died when my father was just five years old—a reminder of how much so much of America's history is buried.*

One thing that hasn't changed for me as a result of this revelation is my Catholic heritage. I am a believing and practicing Catholic, married to another believing and practicing Catholic. And being an American Catholic at this particular moment in history has three particular implications for my own point of view as a candidate for the presidency.

The first two follow directly from the two great commandments set forth in the Scriptures: our obligations to love God with all our hearts, souls, and minds and to love our neighbors as ourselves. The first commandment means we must believe that there are absolute standards of right and wrong. They may not always be that clear, but they exist, and it is our duty to honor them as best we can.

The second commandment means that our commitment to equal rights and social justice, here and around the world, is not simply a matter of political fashion or economic and social theory but a direct command from God. From this perspective "Christian" bigotry and intolerance are nothing less than a direct affront to God's law and a rejection of God's love.

There's a third facet of being an American Catholic that I take very seriously. We've always been a minority in this country, and have sometimes suffered persecution. To a larger extent than Catholics elsewhere, we have supported and relied upon the constitutional principle of the separation of church and state to guarantee our right to worship and our liberty of conscience. That tradition, strongly advanced by John Kennedy in his quest to become our first Catholic president, helped make religious affiliation a nonissue in American politics. It should stay that way.

Democrats and Republicans must also take a long look at our recent tendency to compete in a politics of personal self-interest.

It's really become an anomaly. Just about every Democratic activist or elected official I've ever known entered politics out of a belief in principle and in progress for all, not just for some. We're by tradition the party that actually upholds collective action through government as essential to build a true commonwealth, as well as to defend individual liberties and create individual opportunity. One of our central goals is to convince people to think beyond their own selfish interests and accept the responsibilities of citizenship and the mission of spreading freedom and democracy.

Yet in recent election cycles Democrats have tried to compete with Republicans in a bidding war to see who can shower voters with the greater share of the public treasury: our prescription drug benefits versus their tax cuts; our teacher salaries versus their vouchers; our stuff versus their stuff. We've managed to join the Republicans in an effort to convince the citizens of the proudest nation on earth to conduct a personal cost-benefit analysis of their relationship with government and to view elections as a chance to cut a better deal.

I think this is a betrayal of Democratic principle, and it, too, is self-defeating. We can never beat today's Republicans in appeals to selfishness.

At the core of Republicans' purpose and policies is a big step backward toward their late-nineteenth-century tradition of social Darwinisim, elitism, and the celebration of economic privilege as part of the natural order of things. Even in their rare "compassionate" moments, today's Republicans often offer charity instead of genuine opportunity or justice. They express sympathy for the less privileged with a spirit of pity for life's losers instead of solidarity for fellow citizens who deserve the chance to gain a position in the winner's circle.

My campaign will refuse to play the "what's in it for

me?" game. Instead, we will put our message where our hearts are: asking the American people to join us in a citizens' campaign to make this country as strong, prosperous, wise, and bighearted as we know it can be.

On every major political issue, we should ask Americans to frame key political questions not in terms of what's in it for them but what's in it for all of us.

We should ask Americans to think of the federal budget not as a dispenser of benefits and a confiscator of wealth but as a balance sheet of investments that we as a people have decided are important enough to tax ourselves to make.

We should ask Americans to think of our foreign policy not just as a projection of our influence and our military power but of our principles and our freedoms.

We should ask Americans to think of the impending crisis in the Social Security and Medicare system not as a problem affecting the pocketbooks of seniors but as an intergenerational challenge to our willingness to lay aside a portion of our wealth for future needs we know that we will soon have.

We should ask Americans to think of energy policy not just in immediate terms of pump prices but in terms of our standing in the world and our capacity to sustain economic growth while preserving our environment at home.

And we should ask Americans to think of our civil liberties not as rights to be defended only when it is convenient and ignored when it is not but as essential to who we are.

If we can begin to get our fellow citizens to look at the world—at *their* world—from a fundamentally patriotic perspective on domestic as well as international issues, the difference between Democrats and Republicans will become unmistakably clear and so will the choices in 2004.

There's one other element of our Democratic heritage that I want to reclaim to make it clear just how much we differ from Republicans: our heritage as the party of reform.

Republicans typically don't care how effective domestic government programs are because as a matter of principle they don't believe in domestic government. But Democrats must be scrupulously concerned about the results we get for the taxpayer dollars we invest. We should be passionately involved not just to ensure that well-intentioned programs have the resources they need to succeed but that success is achieved in measurable ways. Across the entire domestic agenda, Democrats should welcome and champion new ideas, not distrust change as a threat to the familiar status quo.

For example, I've been a passionate advocate of reforming our public schools during my Senate career. And it bothers me that some Democrats have resisted the idea of making educational outcomes—the skills and knowledge our kids obtain from the educational system—as important as educational inputs—the adequate funding, the good facilities, and the higher teacher pay we all want.

In every area of government, we should be the first to demand demonstrable results, because we are the first to claim that the public sector can get results. But we should never confuse government as an organizer of public resources with government as an owner-operator of public enterprises. Some areas, like public schools and the police, are properly the province of the public sector. We can't strengthen education by weakening public education. But there are countless areas—child care, after-school programs, environmental protection—where government can and should work through community organizations, nonprofit, and even for-profit private enterprises or public-private partnerships.

Most of all, I believe we should respond to Republican attacks on government not simply by defending it, warts and all, but by reforming government to achieve the best possible results through the most efficient means and the freshest ideas. The great progressives of the past—FDR, JFK, LBJ—did not envision the New Deal, the New Frontier, or the Great Society as perfect or permanent accomplishments. If we are to be called progressives, we must rekindle the innovative spirit that created the best government initiatives, not worship the dead letter of their programmatic residue.

The reinventing government movement of the 1990s needs to be revived—and, indeed, it is already being revived by governors, mayors, and county executives whose revenue windfalls of the Clinton boom have been replaced by the hard fiscal times of the Bush bust. At every level of government, we need to find ways to reduce bureaucracy, focus on results, distinguish high priorities from low ones, and deploy technology to achieve more with less.

If we stop defending the bad things about government, we will no longer risk losing the argument to Republicans, who want to throw out the good with the bad and pare back public investments across the board.

Our reform agenda must include not only government programs but also our democratic system itself. The time has come for us to be ashamed of living in the country with the lowest voting participation and the highest campaign spending of any advanced democratic society. As the international controversy over our confrontation with Iraq has shown, people in other democracies, which have much higher voting rates, have logically wondered if the Bush administration's hard line truly reflects the large majority of voting-age Americans who did not vote for George W. Bush.

Unlike ideologues on the left or the right, I'm not confident that I know for a fact that nonvoters ultimately favor one party or another. But I do know I'd be more confident in making that judgment if voting rates rose to European levels. And as I have repeatedly said, my campaign will focus on mobilizing nonvoters, in part because it's the right thing to do, and in part because I don't want to be a president like our current one, whose "mandate" comes from a small minority of the American people. And because so many Americans refrain from political and civic involvement because they rightly disapprove of the way campaigns are financed by special interests, I will do everything within my power to work toward a system that includes public financing, full disclosure of contributions, and more civil campaigns.

A campaign that rediscovers our Democratic heritage of common national purpose—that insists on meeting all our country's challenges, domestic and foreign; that engages all citizens equally in that task; and that makes government an instrument of the popular will—will give Democrats and the independents we seek to attract the best and highest ground for taking on the Republican Party and the Bush administration.

I believe that, as a candidate for the presidency, I may confidently put my values; my record in public life; my knowledge of how the world works, from international and military affairs to small business to family life; and my agenda for what America can become up against anyone else's.

I don't really care about labels. If I'm dismissed by Republicans or conservative media as a Massachusetts liberal or attacked by Democratic rivals or liberal media as a Clinton-style centrist, I will simply state my values and my ideas and let the voters make their own decisions.

The progressive tradition that I claim is not exclusively the province of either political party or of the political left or right. It was expressed more than 140 years ago by Abraham Lincoln, who told his first wartime Congress this: "The dogmas of the quiet past are inadequate to the stormy present. The occasion is piled high with difficulty, and we must rise with the occasion. As our case is new, so we must think anew, and act anew." That same tradition was championed by one of my predecessors as a senator from Massachusetts, whose younger brother is my senior colleague and a continuing influence on my conscience and my agenda. In accepting the Democratic nomination for the presidency in 1960, John Kennedy did not tell people what government would do for them. Instead he called the nation to a higher standard: "The New Frontier of which I speak is not a set of promises—it is a set of challenges. It sums up not what I intend to offer the American people but what I intend to ask of them. It appeals to their pride, not their pocketbook—it holds out the promise of more sacrifice instead of more security."

It's that spirit that Democrats need to lead the country and that America needs to lead the world. We must stand for the courage to challenge and the vision to lead.

The Bush administration, for all its claims about the necessity of fighting terrorists overseas, has a timid, unimaginative, and fundamentally reactionary agenda for America that will make us selfish and second-rate at a time when we should be united and great.

We have the means and the opportunity in this country to create the highest standard of living the world has ever seen. We have the brainpower to clean up our environment, improve our quality of life, spread innovation throughout our workplaces, build twenty-first-century schools, give Americans longer life and better health, eradicate bigotry, and radically reduce poverty. And we can spread political and economic freedom around the world, doing so in a way that makes America the most admired, not the most feared, nation on earth.

I believe I've been called to service in 2004, as I hope this book will make clear in addressing six big challenges facing our country in the decade ahead. Please read what I've written here, think, argue, and consider. Beyond these pages, Teresa and I will make ourselves an open book and offer a clear proposition for national leadership. Read us as well, then join us in answering the call to service and taking the opportunity we have in 2004 to turn this country around.

Together, we can live up to the patriotism and courage Americans show every day and make America the living proof of the possibilities of the human spirit that were the divine inspiration of our Founders—and of true leaders today.

The Challenge of Protecting America and Promoting Its Values and Interests

★

The title of this chapter is a mouthful. But it's important to convey this idea fully and accurately: We cannot keep Americans safe from violence from abroad if we do not also aggressively and imaginatively make the world safe for our values of political and economic freedom and for our strategic national interests as well.

It's also important for us to keep the international challenge in perspective. Thanks to the sacrifices at home, abroad, and in battle of many millions of Americans and of our allies on five continents, the totalitarian threats of the twentieth century were finally defeated. But while victory was the work of many hands, the institutions and policies that emerged from the struggles against fascism and communism bore our country's distinctive hallmarks: generous treatment of the vanquished, a commitment to human rights and democracy, and a multilateral approach to addressing common problems and resolving conflicts. Americans should take pride in the leadership we exercised in the creation of the United Nations, the Bretton Woods family of international economic institutions, and a whole host of official and public-private human rights and development programs.

Thanks to American leadership, the world today has a strong democratic core—so strong that even protesters against globalization share many of the values that underlie the policies they deplore. But on the periphery of the world are unstable and dangerous places, places where terrorists, absolutists, neo-Fascists, and gangsters work to undo the twentieth century and impose a new dark age. Though these forces are essentially weak and defensive and far less popular even in their home territories than the American values they oppose, they have repeatedly demonstrated the global reach of their ability to do violence.

The proliferation of international criminal gangs and narco-terrorists in the 1990s—a subject I wrote about in my 1997 book, *The New War*—was a warning that we were no longer safe at home from the dark underside of a global society. Any lingering doubt about that reality was dramatically dispelled on 9/11.

Our challenge is to expand the twentieth-century consensus that political freedom is the best guarantor of human rights and that economic freedom is the best engine for prosperity. This is a challenge we can meet if we call upon every resource at our disposal, including the power of our ideas and the willingness of much of the world to embrace them. Indeed, the extremism of our enemies is an indication of their desperate understanding of the ultimate appeal of our values.

The president has used our armed forces since 9/11, but he has routinely and inexcusably failed to draw upon our other international assets, including our values, our alliances, and the multilateral organizations we largely created. By limiting its foreign policy to military responses, the Bush administration sells America short and leaves us more vulnerable than we should be.

Our overthrow of the Taliban regime in Afghanistan and Saddam Hussein in Iraq were stunning reaffirmations of the unequalled prowess of the U.S. armed forces. I fear they will prove to be hollow victories, however, unless we have an administration that knows how to match force with diplomacy and create a long-range strategy for collective security, the rule of international law, and the spread of democracy throughout the world.

As a country we now face a choice that we faced many times during the last century—between isolation in a perilous world and engagement to shape the world. We've always embraced the latter but sometimes only after risking great damage to our safety and our interests.

Today's harsh conservative unilateralism is no better than the right's old isolationist impulse. It's aggressive only when the opportunity for military action beckons. At its core is a familiar and beguiling illusion: that America can escape entanglement with the world and wield its enormous power without incurring obligations to others, that it can, in effect, advance its values and protect its interests without friends and allies.

The blustering behavior of the Bush administration toward friends and enemies alike has been a keystone of its foreign policy practically from the moment of the president's inauguration and has been its response in almost every circumstance. That attitude is not just an unpleasant by-product of the fight against terrorists but a fundamental diplomatic misconception that if not corrected will limit our global influence to those goals we can reach by force and intimidation alone—and even they will be at risk if we do not share the burdens of the effort to achieve them.

The president and many of his advisers have forgotten that genuine global leadership is a strategic imperative for America, not a favor we do for other countries. Leading the world's most advanced democracies isn't a matter of mushy multilateralism; it amplifies America's voice and extends its reach. Working through global institutions doesn't tie our hands; it invests our aims with greater legitimacy, brings us vital support, and dampens the resentment that great power inevitably inspires.

In a world growing more interdependent every day, unilateralism is a formula for crippling isolation and shrinking influence. As much as some in the White House may desire it, America can't opt out of a networked world or simply log in and out of it when the situation suits us. Those who seek to lead have a duty to offer not only a clear vision of how we can make Americans safer but also how we can make America itself more trusted and respected in the world.

That's definitely true of all of us who are asking the American people to replace President Bush.

One of the reasons I'm running for president is to oppose a Democratic trend—sadly reminiscent of a similar movement in the 1970s and 1980s—to concede international and security issues to the opposition party and constantly try to focus campaigns on domestic issues. Fed by the all-too-conventional wisdom of consultants, pollsters, and strategists, this domestic-only strategy shows contempt for the heightened security concerns of our citizens, abandons a rich history of Democratic internationalism, and, worst of all, leaves the dangerous foreign policy and national security views of the Republican Party unchallenged.

My own training as a Democratic internationalist began in early childhood. I was a foreign service brat, which is a lot like growing up as an Army brat or a Navy brat, except that the PX privileges aren't as good. The experience was valuable in two important respects: Spending a good chunk of your childhood overseas exposes you to a lot of other cultures, languages, political traditions, and histories. And it also teaches you a lot about what America distinctively stands for and what much of the world depends on us to stand for.

My most compelling memory of my time as a foreign service brat was a walk I took with my father on the beaches of Normandy, where thousands of young Americans died fighting for freedom. As my father pointed to burned-out bunkers, the casings of exploded shells, and the skeletons of landing vehicles, I came face to face, at an early age, with the true meaning of national sacrifice. I think that that beach, where thousands died for a freedom we continue to defend today, is one of the most powerful symbols of how my father and the greatest generation answered the challenges of their era. They had the courage to win a world war, and they didn't stop there; they went further and secured the peace, rebuilding Europe and setting the stage to win the cold war.

Like all foreign service officers, my father was often transferred. He was legal adviser to the American mission in Berlin in the mid-1950s, spent time at the NATO War College, and was political secretary to our embassy in Norway for four years before retiring from the foreign service in 1962, when I had already started college. One assignment that he had in Washington that made an especially strong impression on me was when he was briefly detailed to the staff of the Senate Foreign Relations Committee. It was with a sense of continuing a family tradition that I appeared before that same committee in 1971 after my service in Vietnam, testifying on behalf of the Vietnam Veterans Against the War. And when I was elected to the U.S. Senate in 1984, I fought with my staff for three solid days over my wish to serve on the Foreign Relations Committee. They had gotten some assurances in Washington, God knows how, that I had a chance, rare for a freshman, to get a seat on Appropriations, that great horn of plenty for home state projects and reelection politics. But I was determined to get on Foreign Relations, and I've been a member ever since.

My experiences on that committee over the course of nearly twenty years have continually strengthened my belief that Democrats need to remember that it was our party that laid the foundations for our country's current preeminence, built the institutions through which American power and prestige spanned the globe, and wrote the book on engagement with the world. Republicans sometimes seem to want to believe that the cold war began and ended with Ronald Reagan. The best way to keep the record straight is to reaffirm our own internationalist tradition and its remarkable vision of a world where our values are admired, our interests are shared, and our leadership is respected.

Our tradition is defined by the tough-minded strategy of international engagement and leadership forged by Wilson and Roosevelt in two world wars and championed by Truman and Kennedy in the cold war. They recognized that America's security depended not on going it alone but on our capacity to rally the forces of freedom. And they understood that to make the world safe for democracy, diversity, and individual liberty, we needed to build international institutions dedicated to establishing the rule of law over totalitarianism and anarchy. That's why Roosevelt pushed hard for the United Nations, the World Bank, and the IMF.

It's why Truman insisted not only on creating NATO and resisting Communist insurgencies but also on the Marshall Plan to speed Europe's recovery. It's why Kennedy not only faced down the Soviet Union over nuclear missiles in Cuba but also signed the Nuclear Test Ban Treaty and launched the Peace Corps.

The time has come to renew that tradition, and revive a bold vision of progressive internationalism for the twenty-first century. Our country and our party need to engage in a dialogue about all the things that will make us stronger. I believe there is a better vision for how we deal with the rest of the world, a better vision for how we build relationships, a better vision for how we structure our military forces, a better vision for how we fight a war and win it, and a better vision for accepting the responsibility of being the sole superpower in the world.

Woodrow Wilson was elected during peace; he led during war. Franklin Roosevelt was elected to tackle the Great Depression and put America back to work, but soon had to respond to Pearl Harbor and marshal the nation's might from Normandy to Iwo Jima. And John Kennedy didn't try to change the subject of the debate when General Eisenhower's vice president brought up foreign policy. He challenged America globally—insisting that we do more and that we do certain things not because they were easy but because they were hard.

That is the standard of leadership, engagement, and vision that defines our party and that must now be our standard if we are to lead this nation once again.

Remember that the president has three key responsibilities in his job description: chief executive of the fiscal and domestic policies of the United States, head of state and therefore the nation's chief diplomat, and commander in chief of the nation's military forces. We dare not avoid discussing two-thirds of the job.

Democrats can and must offer an alternative to the Bush administration's contemptuous unilateralism and its inability to deploy effectively the tools of diplomacy as it does those of war. At the same time, we cannot let our national security agenda be defined by those who reflexively oppose any U.S. military intervention anywhere as a repetition of Vietnam and who see U.S. power as mostly a malignant force in world politics. The minimum we should ask of the next Democratic nominee for president is someone who was at least as critical of French and Russian obstructionism in the UN during the debate on Iraq as of the Bush administration's reluctance to go to the UN and its disdain for the idea of a broad international coalition. And I don't think we have a prayer of regaining the White House if our candidate seems weak, inexperienced, or unsure on national security.

I'm often asked how my military service in Vietnam—and my later involvement with Vietnam Veterans Against the War—affect my views today on these great issues of war and peace and American leadership.

I learned a lot in Vietnam, much of it about the courage and honor of my brothers-in-arms and, through them, the honorable intentions of the American people from whom they were drawn. I could never agree with those in the antiwar movement who dismissed our troops as war criminals or our country as the villain in the drama. That's one reason, in fact, that I eventually parted ways with the VVAW organizations and instead helped found the Vietnam Veterans of America.

But serving in Vietnam did confirm my belief that the war itself was a colossal mistake—not because there was anything ignoble about opposing the expansion of communism in Southeast Asia but because we had intervened in a civil war to fight for a corrupt and undemocratic regime in Saigon. The lesson I learned from Vietnam is that you quickly get into trouble if you let foreign policy or national security policy get too far adrift from our values as a country and as a people. We knew whom we were fighting against during those patrols on the Mekong Delta but did not really know what we were fighting for.

I'm afraid some of our leaders learned the wrong lessons from that war. Many conservatives along with many military professionals decided after Vietnam that wars should be fought only with full public support, the certainty of victory, and by using overwhelming force to gain a quick decision. Conservative support for brutal right-wing death squads in Central America during the 1980s may have reflected a false belief that excessive restraint was the cause of our failure in Vietnam.

I fully support the concept of a quick victory when war is deemed unavoidable, but we cannot always choose our opponents for their weakness. Use of force sometimes has to be controversial and limited. And we are dangerously distant from our moorings as a nation if we make military or political considerations alone the reason for using or not using force. I supported our military intervention in Kosovo, which was both controversial and limited, though ultimately successful. Many conservative supporters of the Powell Doctrine, including its namesake, opposed this action. But it proved to be the right thing to do in the face of potential genocide and given a carefully weighed proportionate use of force.

There are also leaders on the left and among the Democrats who learned a different wrong lesson from Vietnam: that U.S. military action is rarely if ever justified and usually reflects misguided arrogance or bumbling interference in other countries' affairs. That extrapolation from the experience of Vietnam denies all the good the United States did earlier in the twentieth century by force of arms to end the slaughter of World War I and the imperial rivalries that fueled it, to halt fascism in World War II, and to resist the spread of totalitarian communism before and after Vietnam. Moreover, this "Vietnam syndrome" brought into the progressive movement and the Democratic Party an unfortunate receptiveness to a "blame America" interpretation of world events that is untrue to the facts, unfair to our country, and unworthy of those who claim to share a commitment to freedom and human rights, which have often required the active and sometimes armed support of the United States.

As a veteran of both the Vietnam War and the Vietnam protest movement, I say to both conservative and liberal misinterpreters of that war that it's time to get over it and recognize it as an exception, not as a ruling example, of the U.S. military engagements of the twentieth century. If those of us who carried the physical and emotional burdens of that conflict can regain perspective and move on, so can those whose involvement was vicarious or who know nothing of the war other than ideology and legend.

✫

Americans deserve better than a false choice between force without diplomacy and diplomacy without force. They deserve a principled diplomacy, backed by military might, based on enlightened self-interest rather than the short-sighted pursuit of power—a diplomacy that commits America to lead in many different ways, not just with force but not always without it, toward a world of greater liberty and more widely shared prosperity, with the substantial cooperation of friends and allies.

To appreciate fully the imperative of diplomacy in today's world requires a deeper sense of the nature and source of the threat we face. While we must remain determined to defeat terrorism, it isn't only terrorism we are fighting, it's also the beliefs that motivate terrorists and the conditions that make those beliefs possible.

If you look at the countries stretching from Morocco through the Middle East and beyond—broadly speaking, the western Muslim world—what you see is a civilization under extraordinary political, economic, and cultural stress. According to Freedom House, there are no full-fledged democracies among the sixteen Arab states of the Middle East and North Africa. Jordan, Morocco, and Qatar are making progress, but Israel remains the only Middle Eastern democracy. Political and economic participation by Arab women remains the lowest in the world. More than half of Arab women are still illiterate. Public education in most of these nations is still tainted by distortions and ethnic and religious hatreds.

These countries are also among the most economically isolated in the world, with very little trade and investment and little income apart from the oil royalties that flow to the ruling elites. They generally don't trade with one another; most of them don't trade with Israel, the Middle East's economic dynamo; and they don't trade much with the rest of the world, other than in oil. Since 1980 the share of world trade held by the fifty-seven member countries of the Organization of the Islamic Conference (OIC) has fallen from 15 percent to just 4 percent. The same fifty-seven countries attracted only $13.6 billion in foreign direct investment in 2001. That's just a bit more than the investment attracted by Sweden, whose population is nine million, while the OIC countries have a population of 1.3 billion. As an example of the stagnation endemic to the region, consider that Egypt and South Korea had roughly equal gross domestic products back in 1969. Egypt has scarcely grown since then, while South Korea has become one of the twenty largest economies in the world.

With a landscape marked by political oppression, economic stagnation, staggering unemployment levels, lack of education, poverty, refusal to integrate women into the workforce, and rapid population growth, is it any wonder these Islamic countries are recruiting grounds for terrorists?

While we must obviously continue to hunt down and destroy terrorist networks harbored in the Middle East and

demand cooperation from every regime in the region, we
need more than a one-dimensional war on terror. We must
engage in a smarter, more comprehensive, and more far-
sighted strategy for modernizing the greater Middle East.
It's no more ambitious—and no less necessary—a task than
the rebuilding of Europe that we undertook at the end of
World War II.

Reopening Middle Eastern economies is an especially
urgent priority. If we aren't proactive about stimulating
nonpetroleum trade with and within the region, the situation is likely to get worse, not better. For one thing, existing U.S. trade preferences for countries in Africa, Central
America, the Caribbean, and South Africa may divert and
diminish what little trade we already have with the Middle
East.

We should act quickly to expand the kinds of tariff-
free trade policy we extended in the African Growth and
Opportunity Act—which doubled manufacturing exports
to the United States during the last three years—to the
greater Middle East. To qualify, these countries should
agree to drop their economic boycott of Israel, end all support for terrorists, and respect basic worker rights and environmental principles, as Jordan did in the bilateral trade
agreement with the United States negotiated by the Clinton administration. That United States–Jordan agreement
expanded Jordanian exports to the United States from sixteen million dollars to four hundred million dollars almost
overnight, creating forty thousand jobs. It would be won-
derful to see that kind of economic growth flourish next

door in a peaceful and democratic Palestinian state that would send goods, not suicide bombers, to Israel.

The president endorsed a move in this direction in May of 2003, but his proposal was aimed mainly at the distant prospect of a regional free trade agreement some decades down the road. The area needs economic help, and its people need opportunity immediately.

As majority-Islamic countries outside the Middle East have demonstrated, there's no inherent conflict between faith in Islam and growth in trade. In Europe, Turkey, Albania, and Bosnia have actively sought economic integration with the West. In Southeast Asia, other majority-Muslim nations like Brunei, Indonesia, and Malaysia are large exporters and active members of the World Trade Organization.

The urgency of building a modern economy in Iraq should provide the impetus for a regionwide effort, led by the United States and supported by international institutions like the World Bank and the IMF, to liberalize regimes and reform economies. Our long-term goal must be to help these countries build democratic institutions, their best chance for peace and prosperity.

This requires that the United States reengage with the world community, with Arab and Islamic countries, and with our past and present European allies. As of this writing, it's clear the administration seems determined to rebuild Iraq with only minimal involvement by the UN and the international community. This approach compounds the mistake made in postwar Afghanistan of relying strictly on peacekeeping forces and indigenous regional chieftains to impose order. Going down that path can lead to new dictators, civil wars, and failed states. A multilateral and multidimensional strategy is the only one that offers lasting hope for a prosperous, stable, democratic Iraq, which itself can then contribute to the political and economic progress of the entire Middle East.

We could argue at length—and historians may argue for years—about the impact of the Bush administration's long pattern of unilateralism, which was manifested so strikingly in the narrow coalition assembled against Saddam Hussein and in the strong anti-American feelings so evident around the world since the Bush administration came to power. There's no doubt at all, however, that far more effective diplomacy is now needed to reestablish U.S. leadership in the world community, rebuild and retool damaged multilateral institutions, and reengage allies in the common work of fighting terrorism, expanding freedom, and building democracy.

There have been periods in our history when it didn't much matter if we had a president who was inclined toward fostering international relations or commanded a lot of personal respect in other countries. This is emphatically not one of those times. It is hard to think of a modern presidency so reflexively and systematically marked by rejection of diplomacy, international cooperation, and other building blocks for collective security as that of George W. Bush. The first sign of indifference was the summary rejection of the Kyoto Protocol on Global Climate Change, the handiwork of dozens of countries acting under U.S. leadership for a decade. Kyoto could and should have been improved; instead, it was dismissed by the Bush government out of hand. This was followed by the United States's refusal to sign the Comprehensive Test Ban Treaty, another product of long years of American leadership. Both rejections came in the president's first year in office.

Much of the prestige and influence the Bush administration sacrificed in that first year was replenished by a great wave of world sympathy for the United States after 9/11. But even that was drained away by a series of administration actions, beginning with the announcement of an expanded right of preemption that would extend beyond imminent threats and grant the United States a unique sanction to strike against any potential enemy—with a dangerously vague and broad definition of the term "enemy"—at any time. It looked for a while as if the president was going to exercise that "right" against Iraq without so much as a discussion with the United Nations. In fact, that might have happened had not congressional Democrats insisted on a debate on the use of force and then forced the administration to take its case to the UN Security Council.

We'll never know if a more patient and inclusive diplomatic effort by an administration with better international credentials would have succeeded in obtaining Security Council support or at least acceptance of the United States–led coalition to disarm Saddam. But it should be clear as a result of that experience that we need to make an all-out effort to rebuild our collective security institutions, including the UN and NATO, unless we want them to wither away or become the focal point for anti–United States intrigues. And we must immediately form a coalition of allies to become involved in the difficult task of rebuilding Iraq, a challenge that the Bush administration clearly underestimated.

There's one thing you cannot take away from President Bush: He did establish beyond a shadow of a doubt the credibility of U.S. threats to use military force against our enemies. Our strength is a national asset, but it's an asset that will decline steadily unless it's matched with others, including the willingness and skill to use diplomacy and the institutions of collective security to protect our nation and its interests without constant war. It's precisely these peaceful assets that the Bush administration appears determined to squander or ignore.

The Bush administration is by no means the only culprit in the breakdown in U.S.–UN relations over Iraq. France, Germany, and Russia never supported or offered a feasible policy to verify that UN resolutions on Iraq were actually being carried out. And it's clear that France is flirting with a revival of Charles de Gaulle's fantasy of making Europe an independent counterweight to U.S. power, led, of course, from Paris. As far as Germany is concerned, the neopacifism that underlay its objections to military action against Saddam threatens to make NATO toothless and irrelevant as an instrument for the collective security of the Atlantic Alliance. Yet our core relationship with Germany thankfully remains strong, and our stake in NATO clear and compelling as ever.

America's interests clearly call for a return to multi-lateralism and a serious effort to make it effective. If there wasn't a UN, we'd have to invent a comparable institution as an instrument for conferring the legitimacy of the world community on a wide variety of military, economic, and humanitarian endeavors. And so long as the United States and Europe, along with Japan, remain the primary advocates for democracy and liberal capitalism in the world, a regional security agreement like NATO continues to be essential, though its future mission urgently needs to be clarified.

To put it another way, the United States has poured generations of talent and treasure into these institutions, and rather than abandoning or downgrading them, we should refashion and strengthen them for a new generation of service to the world. Our British, Spanish, and Eastern European coalition allies are eager to rebuild European unity. Moreover, Europeans arguably need the kind of collective security offered by NATO and the UN more than we do, since they would otherwise be forced to drastically increase their own defense spending or accept a permanent posture of appeasement toward each successive threat on the horizon.

I hope by the time you read this book that the UN has been usefully employed as a partner in the reconstruction of Iraq and that Jacques Chirac has ceased his foolish rebellion against the very idea of the Atlantic Alliance. America, which has always shown magnanimity in victory, should in turn meet repenting Europeans more than halfway, not ratchet up the badgering unilateralism that fed European fears in the first place.

UN and European help will also be critical to our success in the Middle East peace process, which, after two and a half years of alternating indifference and fumbling intervention, the Bush administration has finally resumed.

Israel is our ally, for it is not just the only real democracy in the Middle East but a bulwark of U.S. security in a region rife with threats. Its future can be best assured over the long term only if real and lasting peace can be brought to its entire neighborhood. I know from my own trips to Israel that despite the painful experiences of the last several years, the majority of the Israeli people accept the ultimate establishment of a Palestinian state. But, ironically enough, they are unsure whether the Palestinian leadership will ever accept such a state if it also means accepting a Jewish state with secure boundaries. Yasir Arafat's summary rejection of the Clinton and Barak proposals in 2000 stunned most Israelis. His actions not only spelled an end to the Oslo peace process but also politically discredited its Israeli proponents. Moreover, the involvement of Arafat's own Fatah organization in terrorist acts—including suicide bombings—during the ensuing second intifada served only to underscore his many years of association with terrorism before Oslo, making him an impossible peace partner for Israel.

That's why the best news for Middle Eastern peace is the rise of a new group of Palestinian leaders that seems committed to give a fresh start to the peace process. European nations, which have supplied the Palestinian Authority with both funding and international credibility, have a special responsibility to guide the political evolution of the Palestinians in the right direction.

The road map for Middle East peace recently proposed by the United States, the UN, Russia, and the European Union lays out the main steps to peace: Palestinian renunciation of terror and suppression of terrorist groups, along with democratization of its own institutions; Israeli military withdrawal to preintifada lines, suppression of illegal settlements and suspension of new settlement activity; and a mutual return to negotiations over borders and other final status issues.

But the biggest step each side must take is not really explicitly addressed in that road map. For Palestinians, it's compromising on the "right to return" to Israel, since that claim inherently rejects the establishment of the Jewish state in Palestine in 1948. For Israelis, the test is extending truly equal rights and equal services to non-Jewish citizens—and once terrorism has ended and secure boundaries have been set, creating a genuine economic partnership with an independent Palestine.

While the United States should recognize that both parties must be willing to walk the path to peace together, we must also acknowledge there is no substitute for our own leadership in lighting that path and dealing with potential pitfalls all along the way.

If I'm elected president, I won't make the mistake of having only intermittent involvement in the Middle East. And I will make certain that our unshakable commitment to Israel's existence as a Jewish state within secure boundaries is never forgotten or misunderstood anywhere in the region. When a potential even if flawed breakthrough for peace appears, like the 2002 initiative by the Saudi crown prince Abdullah, I will personally act to make sure the impetus is not lost. First 9/11 and now events in Iraq have created a very different political dynamic in the Arab world. It can work strongly for peace or ultimately against it. State-sponsored support for terrorism against Israel simply must end, along with the double standards of Arab regimes that hedge public support for the war on terrorism with private subsidies for anti-Western Islamic radicalism. Al Qaeda attacks on Saudi Arabia and other Muslim countries make it abundantly clear we are all in this fight together.

In running for president, I am acutely aware of the power of the United States at this particular moment of history. It means the leader of our country has an astonishing amount of power to do good or evil around the world—not just by major acts of war, peace or diplomacy but minor policy decisions and even simply by what issues he seems to care about or not care about. The next president of the

United States will have much more power than his predecessors, like Richard Nixon, whose policies I largely opposed, or Jimmy Carter, whose foreign policies for the most part I supported.

I know President Bush understands his power as commander in chief of the strongest military in the history of the world, though I'm less convinced that he understands his power as leader of the most successful society in the history of the world. If he did, I suspect he would not squander it so often. The president has missed major opportunities to address the downside of globalization by advancing its upside—with help for nations around the globe struggling against environmental degradation and global health crises and with measures like debt relief in exchange for better development policies and improved trade relationships. We need to show the world the face of enlightened—not Enron—capitalism. British Prime Minister Tony Blair has been eloquent and insistent about accepting this challenge. We need a president who will be an unsilent partner with them in creating a vision for the twenty-first century that offers hope to those left out of the blessings of a modern economy and builds allies for Western leadership and Western values. We should be the world's leader in sustainable development. We should be the world's leader in technology transfer and technical assistance to meet a host of environmental and health problems.

And we also need a president who doesn't do the right thing for the wrong reasons. Last year Republican Senator Bill Frist of Tennessee and I sponsored a bill to make control of the AIDS epidemic in Africa—and humanitarian relief for the twenty-nine million victims afflicted there—a foreign policy and budget priority for the United States. The administration offered no support at all and actively opposed appropriations for this purpose.

A few months later, Senate Republican leader Trent Lott re-signed his leadership position after a controversy over his enthusias-tic comments about the 1948 segregationist presidential candidacy of the since-deceased Strom Thurmond. Senator Frist succeeded Lott as majority leader, and the president, apparently as sort of a graduation present, agreed to support a version of our AIDS pack-age in his 2003 State of the Union Address.

I'm grateful the president changed his mind on this subject, though I'm not entirely convinced the administration's commitments on AIDS will ultimately fare any better in the appropriations process controlled by his party in Congress than his earlier broken promise to "leave no child behind."

If I'm elected president, I will use all the power and political capital I can summon to get support from both parties in Congress to do the right thing on broader global challenges like AIDS, world poverty, and the proliferation of dangerous weapons. And I won't hesitate to use the bully pulpit of the Oval Office to mobilize pub-lic support for such policies, either.

It's particularly important that the United States undertake and lead a global and comprehensive effort to deal with proliferation, especially with the threat of nuclear weapons lost or loose in a world where there is a market for them and for the materials to make them. We know that among the customers in this marketplace are not only rogue states like North Korea but terrorist networks like Al Qaeda.

Six years ago authorities seized a nuclear fuel rod that

had been stolen from the Congo. The security guard entrusted with protecting it had simply lent his keys. Two years later, even after this near disaster, the same facility was guarded by only a few underpaid guards, rusty gates, and a simple padlock that could be opened with a single key.

In October 2001 we picked up warnings that terrorists had acquired a ten-kiloton nuclear bomb. If such a device were detonated in New York City, hundreds of thousands of Americans would die and most of Manhattan would be destroyed. After we learned that those rumors were incorrect, my former Senate colleague Sam Nunn issued an important warning: "This intelligence report was judged to be false. But it was never judged to be implausible or impossible."

Unfortunately the Bush administration has made a habit of ignoring Sam Nunn's warnings on a subject in which he is one of the world's preeminent experts. With Dick Lugar, the Republican senator of Indiana who is now chairman of the Senate Foreign Relations Committee, Nunn sponsored a series of initiatives aimed at securing nuclear materials and scientists in the former Soviet Union. Their reasoning, which I share, is that after spending trillions of dollars to win the cold war, it was worth spending a few billion dollars a year to make sure that a stricken former Soviet industry for the production of weapons of mass destruction does not become the source of a fire sale for rogue states and terrorists.

Instead, the Bush administration tried to slash federal funding for these Nunn–Lugar initiatives the moment it took office, an effort it continued well after 9/11 starkly illustrated the potential costs of letting terrorists get control of weapons of mass destruction. More recently the administration has offered more support for Nunn–Lugar initiatives, but we must match that with a broader, multilateral framework for identifying and securing nuclear materials wherever they may be and in whatever quantity. As Nunn and Lugar have long argued, we must help those in possession of deadly materials who lack the financial and technical means to control them to become responsible stewards under international supervision.

The hazards of not paying sufficient attention to proliferation are demonstrated by the crisis we faced with North Korea early in 2003. In that case the Bush administration offered what can only be described as a merry-go-round policy: It got up on its high horse, whooped and hollered, rode around in circles, and ended right back where it started. By suspending talks begun under the Clinton administration, then asking for talks but imposing new conditions, then confirming North Korea's paranoia by identifying Pyongyang as part of the Axis of Evil, then refusing to talk under conditions of nuclear blackmail, then reversing that condition, the administration created a dangerous confusion and let Kim Jong Il make his own crazy carnival interpretation of the situation. After the administration also managed to alienate our key ally in the area, South Korea, it finally wisely decided to back a regional approach to North Korea, engaging China, Japan, and South Korea to put pressure on the North Korean regime to end its nuclear weapons and missile programs. But it has failed to make it clear the United States will take action to fore-stall possible sale of North Korean nuclear materials to other countries or to terrorists—with or without support from other regional players. This is one case where the administration is failing to exercise leadership above and beyond what multilateral organizations can accomplish.

I can make similar arguments about the administration's failures in another key front in the fight against rogue states, terrorist networks, and the potential use of weapons of mass destruction: the home front. The Bush administration denied for a very long time after 9/11 that there was any homeland security challenge at all, beyond the counter-terrorism efforts already being performed by the FBI at home and the CIA overseas. But when polls showed that the public was worried about security against attacks in the United States, the administration abruptly reversed course and embraced a Democratic proposal to create a cabinet-level Department of Homeland Security. Yet the president still did not embrace any real strategy for defending the homeland. What he's offered is little more than a huge new bureaucracy and a run on duct tape. Funding for homeland security's first responders—firefighters, paramedics, and law enforcement—was first delayed, then drawn from other local law-enforcement funding, even as crime rates were rising. The concept of dual-use technology, which would enable local law-enforcement officers to fight crime and terrorism simultaneously, has been completely ignored by the administration and most congressional Republicans.

I've proposed a First Defenders Initiative to help both

firefighters and police staff up against crime and terrorism and give homeland security forces the same degree of support we've given our armed forces overseas. This initiative includes efforts to bring twenty-first century technology to the war on terror so that first defenders can communicate and share lifesaving information. Much of the success of our military's swift advance on Baghdad was due to the remarkable information technology that linked Army and Marine forces on the ground, Navy and Air Force pilots in the sky, Special Ops units behind the lines, and command centers in Kuwait and Washington. We need to give the same kind of capability to those who fight terrorism and crime here at home.

Four of the five terrorists who crashed an airliner into the Pentagon had fake IDs. It's time to create a new generation of "smart" driver's licenses and IDs that use encrypted technology so that they can't be forged. Better, smarter technology can help us focus on real criminal and terrorist suspects instead of pursuing the kind of broad-net violations of civil liberties instituted by Attorney General John Ashcroft.

We should also spur scientists and the private sector to conduct a major effort to create noninvasive technologies to combat terrorism. That means marshaling the nation's greatest scientists to seek and find vaccines, antidotes, and detection technologies to disarm and track down chemical and biological weapons before they can do immense damage.

Many other American resources should also be summoned to the war on terrorism. We should begin by enlisting the National Guard more effectively in homeland security. The AmeriCorps national service program should be expanded to make homeland security one of its core missions, as my colleagues Evan Bayh and John McCain have proposed. And, finally, I think we should create a new Community Defense Service composed of hundreds of thousands of Americans in neighborhoods all over the country. Volunteer service captains would receive training in how to lead their communities in the event of an attack. Community Defense Service units would also identify local health professionals and experts in the area, provide information on local evacuation or quarantine plans, and stand ready to assist first defenders in the hours after an attack. Homeland security was first an afterthought, then a bureaucratic plaything for the current administration. More than ever, keeping America safe is a process that starts at home.

In Vietnam, we had a lot of advantages over our enemies, including better food, better training, better equipment, and better communications systems. But in the firefights in which I was involved, it really came down to fire versus fire, with the enemy employing weapons that could have destroyed us if we hadn't been able to aggressively attack and destroy them first.

Now, thank God, we have superiority against every possible enemy in the air, on land, or at sea, with better technology, more weapons, and better-trained and more skillful troops. This superiority doesn't guarantee success, however, especially if it's undermined by a failure of diplomacy and alliances. But the power we do have, unprecedented in history, is the product of many years of investments and planning by Congress and the executive branch. To an amazing extent, these measures were resisted if not actively opposed by the armed services themselves. For decades, the brass fought technologies and war plans that limited cherished service branch roles in combat or that created greater firepower with more weaponry and less manpower.

From my involvement with defense issues in Congress, I understand why services oppose what has been called the revolution in military affairs, which calls for smaller, more mobile, and more integrated armed forces linked by and using America's enormous technological advantage. But as a former officer in a combat zone, I think we should be focused on making available every possible resource that enables our men and women, regardless of military branch, to achieve their missions with minimum casualties.

In Iraq, Army and Marine units reached Baghdad so quickly with so few casualties not only because of superior communications but because Air Force and Navy air assaults were able to prevent the Iraqi Republican Guards from defending the capital. Ground forces also benefited from an incredible ability to see the enemy, despite sandstorms and the deliberate use of civilians to shield military units. Special Forces behind the lines played a huge role. In other words, we saw impressive proof of the potential of military transformation and, frankly, a repudiation of the tendency by the separate branches and their defenders in Congress to keep the armed forces the way they were when I served in Vietnam.

If I'm elected president, my secretary of state will take on the entrenched interests and I will create an assistant to the president for military transformation to push against the resistance for change. Secretary Rumsfeld failed to follow through over change but he was right to challenge their resistance.

Part of the bargain we make with the brave young men and women who defend us is to take care of them when they come home. America has found many ways to honor its veterans: parades each Memorial Day and Veterans Day, a GI Bill to put higher education within the reach of millions, a commitment to find missing prisoners of war, a variety of benefits, and a growing, towering set of memorials. I have spent a great deal of my time working to help keep the promises America has made to vets. The Army says it never leaves behind its wounded; the Marines say they never leave behind their dead. As a country we need to say we will never leave behind our veterans.

There are a lot of things the Bush administration has done during the president's first terms that I've disagreed with, some quite strongly. The action that most shocked me was the administration-backed effort in Congress to cut veterans' benefits to pay for a new tax cut for the wealthy at the very moment that our men and women in uniform were risking their lives in Iraq. It's not as though vets constitute a luxury class that can easily accommodate a cutback. There are lengthy waiting lists for beds in VA hospitals, and long-suffering vets are still seeking treatment for Gulf war syndrome, the Agent Orange of the 1991 war.

It may sound like political exaggeration to say that the Bush administration cares about our men and women in uniform only when they are on active duty, not before or after they take off the uniform. But that statement is largely true. George W. Bush is a commander in chief who apparently does not understand his duty toward the troops—or their parents, their children, and their fellow-citizens—before or after they are deployed. Thomas Paine famously warned Americans during the Revolutionary War of "summer soldiers" with no allegiance to their country other than their brief periods of service when the country's cause was going well. Now our challenge is to overcome "summer generals" who don't understand that those who serve are an American cause that precedes and succeeds every act of war.

The Challenge of Expanding
Our Common Wealth

★

Over the last three years, the American economy has lost more than three million jobs. Our equity markets have lost four trillion dollars in value. Our private debt has skyrocketed, and our public debt, so recently on the decline, is again rapidly rising. Once-booming and thriving technology corridors are in gloom. Our manufacturing is in freefall. And, sadly, more and more Americans are slipping into poverty. We need action and leadership because we're not just in a temporary downturn; we're in a fight for our economic future.

It's true that the nineties boom slowed down in part because a speculative bubble in technology investment finally burst. And it's also true that 9/11 and the uncertainty over war in Iraq adversely affected consumer and investor confidence. And yes, the economic troubles of other countries, from Asia to Europe to South America, have slowed down international trade and investment. But at some point, it's important that as Americans we stop making excuses for our current condition and start rebuilding the economy that in the past decade gave us the longest period of low-inflation economic growth in our history.

We're the same people we were in the 1990s—just as well-educated, working just as hard, thinking up just as many good ideas. Although the NASDAQ has dropped and many dubious dot-coms have vanished, it's not as if the Information Age has ended. We haven't thrown out our computers and brought back manual typewriters. We haven't forsaken new ways of organizing work and gone back to the hierarchical offices or the dull assembly lines of the past. And the college degrees earned haven't disappeared. What *has* disappeared, however, is the steady expansion of both opportunity and our economy.

We can restore vigorous growth—and the virtuous cycle of higher incomes, lower debt, rising standards of living, and larger investment in the future. But it won't happen by accident or with a president who doesn't know how to unleash the talent and productivity of our people.

I call this chapter "The Challenge of Expanding Our Common Wealth" because we do have to work together to foster the kind of growth we had in the 1990s. Government does not generate wealth; that happens in the private sector. But government does have a crucial if limited role in creating the conditions under which entrepreneurs, innovators, investors, and workers join to generate and sustain growth—and to build the infrastructure and the intellectual capital for projecting that growth into the future.

The Clinton Administration founded its economic strategy on the four pillars: fiscal discipline, open trade, support for innovation, and investment in the knowledge and skills of the American people. The Bush administration has torn down those four pillars one by one and in their place erected a single pillar. This pillar is an idol, really, so fiercely and faithfully is it brought out for every occasion. On it the sum total of the president's fiscal and economic policies have been inscribed: namely, tax cuts for the wealthiest Americans. The idol is a false god, however—useless to the economy, unfair to middle-class taxpayers, and deeply irresponsible to future generations—and we must tear it down.

We cannot go back to the 1990s, and we should not simply restore the Clinton administration's policies. But there are certain bedrock, mainstream principles that can and must power our engines of economic growth:

—Economic growth is built on the talent and hard work of all our people, not just wealthy elites.

—Both private and public investment play a role in building the infrastructure for growth.

—Government must ensure a fair and honest marketplace for business competition, labor-management cooperation, and investors with enforceable standards of integrity for financial

and accounting systems and corporate
executives.

—The progressive system of taxes, which
distributes the burden of self-government in
proportion to the ability to pay, can and
should be maintained without discouraging
enterprise or wealth.

The Bush administration has violated, indeed sometimes even waged war on, all of these foundations of American economic policy.

It has monomaniacally focused on the role of the
wealthy in creating economic growth by inflexibly demanding lower taxes on high earners, big investors, and the
inheritors of huge estates. If the Bush administration has
any long-term economic strategy apart from tax cuts for
this class, I haven't heard about it, and I've definitely been
paying attention. Anyone who has realizes that lower- and
middle-class families have become the forgotten majority
and the passive pawns in the Bush administration's view of
the economy.

Though the president constantly cites the need for private investment in our economy—even while his policies
often undermine investor confidence—his administration
almost never recognizes the role of investment. In their uniform indifference to domestic government, the president

and his supporters shirk investments in quality education, skills training, scientific and technological research, and basic infrastructure projects, including the knowledge-economy infrastructure of high-speed Internet access.

Including Enron and other recent corporate meltdowns, the administration has presided over the worst corporate accountability crisis in living memory. This crisis has damaged not only millions of individual investors but our economy as a whole. The seamy side of corporate conduct on Wall Street is reflected in a growing atmosphere of corporate cronyism in Washington, in which government policies often reward privilege and influence rather than support entrepreneurship and promote competition. It cannot be a complete coincidence that Enron was in line to benefit enormously from administration tax proposals at the same time Enron executives were lining their pockets with insider benefits. And it's no surprise that Republican favoritism towards corporations has been matched by a ferocious hostility to labor unions unseen since the early 1980s.

As well as ignoring these mainstream American economic principles, the Bush administration has consistently violated one principle normally identified with the Republican Party itself, to the detriment of the economy and working families—respect for the role and capacity of state governments. A combination of falling revenues in a slowing economy, rapidly rising health-care costs, reductions in funding for federal-state programs, federal tax cuts affecting state revenue codes, and new responsibilities such as homeland security have the conditions for a perfect storm that has overwhelmed state governments. Aggregate budget shortfalls are approaching one hundred billion dollars for 2003, with no improvement in sight. The nonpartisan National Governors' Association calls it the worst fiscal crisis for states since World War II. As of the spring of 2003, twenty-five governors, many of them Republicans, have proposed state tax increases.

Virtually all states are cutting services and raising fees and taxes (for everything from auto tags to business licenses) wherever they can. Cuts in Medicaid eligibility threaten to increase the already-swollen ranks of Americans without health insurance, at precisely the time when a sluggish economy makes a safety net even more important. States and school districts are struggling to finance the reforms demanded by the federal government in the No Child Left Behind education act, a struggle compounded by the Bush administration's failure to keep the promise of federal funding offered when the initiative was so proudly announced. Many states are imposing double-digit increases in college tuitions at the public institutions most middle-class families rely on, even as a college education is becoming the minimum credential for the jobs of the future. And all these problems are beginning to trickle down to hurt local governments, many of which are raising property taxes.

Even though President Bush is a former governor and won the Republican nomination for president in no small part because other governors supported him, his administration has been remarkably indifferent, if not hostile, to the plight of the states and what that means for mainstream Americans. One of the president's closest allies, the right-wing super-lobbyist Grover Norquist, publicly stated that he hoped at least one state would go bankrupt in order to terrify the others into radically cutting back services. Today's governors are obviously not as fortunate as Governor Bush of Texas was from 1995 to 2000, when the national Clinton-era economic boom swelled his state treasury and made it possible for him to cut taxes while maintaining services—and popularity.

I was elected lieutenant governor of Massachusetts back in 1982, when our economy was in a deep recession and our system of federalism was in real turmoil. Ronald Reagan, under the rubric of New Federalism (a term first used by Lyndon Johnson), was arguing for a wholesale shift of responsibility for many domestic government functions from Washington to the fifty state capitals. I and my small staff spent a lot of time making sure that Massachusetts, which already had its own fiscal problems, did not get crushed by the new burdens unloaded upon it by the federal government.

In the course of this lesson in budgetary defensive driving, I did learn a lot about our system of intergovernmental relations and how different levels of government can act as partners in a way that makes the system more accountable and services more efficient.

I also learned that not all of the Reagan proposals were bad.

He pushed for the consolidation of many tiny, narrow federal-state programs—called categorical grants—that micromanaged the administration of federal dollars at the state and local levels, creating ingrown bureaucracies all down the line. The classic example was a separate transportation program that financed the construction of a bridge but was disconnected from a separate program that financed the maintenance and construction of the highway on both sides of the bridge.

My real lesson as lieutenant governor was that both sides in the New Federalism argument had something to contribute. States do need much greater administrative flexibility in meeting the challenges that the federal government asks them to take on in areas ranging from education and transportation to health care for low-income families, public assistance, environmental protection, and homeland security. But along with that flexibility, states need clear expectations of the results they are accountable for producing and the necessary federal funding to achieve those results. I've tried to continue to support this third way on federal-state relations as a senator.

When you add it up, the Bush administration's economic record is a disaster for most Americans, especially when you consider the economic and fiscal situation this president inherited from Bill Clinton and Al Gore. More than likely, George W. Bush will become the first president since Herbert Hoover to end his first term presiding over an economy with fewer jobs on his last day in office than on his first day. He will definitely end his first term having presided over the most dramatic deterioration in the fiscal condition of the country *ever*—a shift from federal budget surpluses of more than five trillion dollars over ten years to deficits amounting to more than four trillion dollars over ten years, at latest count, with even larger deficits being proposed by the administration as I write these words. Growth will likely be very sluggish, even if 2004 turns out to be a good year.

And perhaps the most surprising fact of all: Despite a one-note domestic agenda of tax cuts and an astonishing indifference to their impact, overall federal-state-local taxes will likely be *higher* for many middle-class families than on the day when George W. Bush took office. With every passing day it's clearer that the administration's tax cuts for privileged Americans will represent a major redistribution of the tax burden from the top to the middle. Meanwhile, out-of-pocket expenses that are critical to working families, including health-care costs, college tuition, and a broad variety of government fees, will be much higher than in 2000.

The first and most important step we need to take to restore our common wealth is to restore fiscal discipline and the progressive principle of taxation. I want to repeal the Bush tax cuts targeted to the wealthiest Americans. That will leave in place tax cuts benefiting the low- to moderate-income Americans who most need the help and who are most likely to spend it in ways that strengthen families and also boost the economy. But repealing the tax cuts for those who are by no definition needy, along with other steps to restrain corporate subsidies and other wasteful spending that I will lay out later in this chapter, will make it possible to stem the tide of budgetary red ink and get us back on the path to a balanced budget and the ability to meet our most pressing national challenges.

And with such measures, I believe we can set a firm goal of reducing the federal budget deficit in half during the next four years.

Cutting the deficit will improve the economy by freeing up capital for private investment and relieving upward pressure on long-term interest rates. But it will also restore our ability to make public investments that contribute to economic growth and a better quality of life.

The administration's pattern of disinvestment in education, training, research, infrastructure, and environmental protection means that within a decade Americans will face the terrible choice of either having to catch up or accepting a lower standard of living. And the trillions of dollars of new public debt this president has created—borrowed, essentially, from the Social Security trust fund—will make it vastly more difficult to deal with the retirement of the baby-boom generation. All these problems, by the way, are being noticed around the world even as they are being ignored or denied in the White House. That means our global economic leadership, so critical to a worldwide economic revival, is being eroded every day George W. Bush remains president.

How do we turn this around? We must think in terms of both short-term and long-term strategies for economic growth.

Our first step has to be to put jobs back at the top of

the national agenda. As president, I will commit this country to turning the tide on manufacturing jobs. I'll start with a tax incentive to encourage companies to keep jobs in America. I will also propose a job-creation tax credit that would give businesses a onetime break from the payroll tax for every new worker they hire. And my health-care plan, which I will explain in a later chapter, will stop spiraling health-care costs, one of the biggest problems facing businesses struggling to maintain employment levels.

Beyond any specific proposals, getting this economy moving again, stopping job losses and creating new jobs depends on a national leadership that believes it can make a difference and can muster the courage and imagination to do so. If elected president, I will hold economic policy summits once a week for the first six months of my administration, aimed at developing targeted strategies to create jobs in key regions and key industries.

Another immediate step we should take is to reverse the damage being done to our economy by the tax increases, education and health-care cuts, and rising college tuition rates being forced on the states by the president's economic and fiscal policies. I will set up a State Tax Relief and Education Fund that will help states struggling to overcome deficits. It will include specific funds for health care to stop cuts that are adding to the ranks of the uninsured and hurting health-care workers, for homeland security to reverse layoffs of "first responders" like police and fire fighters, and for states and school districts to implement the No Child Left Behind education reform initiative.

There's another immediate step we can take to stimulate consumer demand while promoting simple economic justice: increase both the minimum wage and the earned income tax credit, which together create a reasonable floor under the incomes of working families.

Republicans often claim that increasing the minimum wage is a job killer, a burden that businesses cannot afford. What they won't acknowledge is that rising living costs constantly erode the purchasing power of the minimum wage. In fact, you'd have to raise it to $8.14 an hour to give workers the same purchasing power they had in 1969. I believe that the proposal many of us have sponsored in the Senate—to increase the minimum wage to $6.55 an hour—is a modest and reasonable compromise. Then we should index the minimum wage to inflation so that purchasing power is maintained and so that families struggling to get out of poverty don't have to wait for another fight in Congress just to maintain the most basic standard of living.

The earned income tax credit (EITC), which rewards working families for staying off welfare, also needs a boost. That's especially true at a moment when a weak economy is colliding with the time limits on welfare benefits that we enacted in 1996. President Reagan rightly called the EITC the "best antipoverty, the best pro-family, the best job-creation measure to come out of Congress." President Clinton rightly said no family in which parents work full time should have to live in poverty.

Instead of building on the EITC as Presidents Reagan and Clinton suggested, congressional Republicans and some in the Bush administration are waging a war to discourage poor working families from receiving the EITC with the claim that they are fighting fraud. Just last year the IRS announced a plan to make millions of EITC recipients prequalify for their benefits through a separate procedure before claiming the credit on their tax forms. An administration that purports to be compassionate toward the poor and passionate about lowering taxes and reducing bureaucracy is apparently trying to intimidate working families out of benefiting from tax credits by imposing a new layer of bureaucracy—and at the IRS, of all places. Fortunately, Congress forced the administration to postpone this bad idea.

And finally, to spur the economy in the short term, I'd accelerate investments in infrastructure projects, which immediately generate jobs while laying foundations for future growth. Wherever possible, we should aim at double- or triple-dip investments that spur the economy, increase future productivity, and improve our quality of life. What better time to get moving on projects like high-speed rail for commuters and for profitable intercity routes in places including the Boston-Washington corridor and a Portland-Seattle route? Why should we continue to lag behind France and Germany in transportation technology?

Having a clear and compelling strategy for long-term economic growth would also boost short-term consumer and investor confidence and restore confidence around the world in our economic leadership. Indeed, one of the problems we face today is that other countries fear that we are drifting into a Japan-like state of passivity toward our economic problems that could lead to a period of world-wide deflation the likes of which we haven't experienced since the 1930s.

The other critical precondition for reviving the economy and sustaining the revival is the restoration of public confidence in the fairness, integrity, and transparency of our economic system and its accountability to investors, consumers, and workers with a stake in our private enterprises. That means, first and foremost, a federal regulatory system unmistakably on the side of the citizens it represents rather than the corporations it regulates. We also need a president whose approach to corporate abuses is more like Teddy Roosevelt's and less like William McKinley's.

Above all, we need a president who looks our for the well-being of all Americans, fostering broad-based prosperity instead of promoting the interests of those wealthy and powerful interests that hardly need greater representation.

The recent wave of scandals involving corporations, accounting firms, and investment bankers is a replay, only worse, of the series of business disasters that struck in the late 1980s and early 1990s. The savings-and-loan crisis wiped out billions of dollars in savings and required billions of dollars of federal relief to help depositors recover. Even more disturbing were the shadowy dealings of the international bank called BCCI.

I had a front-row seat from which to watch the BCCI scan-

dal unfold. Along with Senator Hank Brown, a Colorado Republican, I led a Senate Foreign Relations Committee investigation of this Arab-owned, Pakistani-operated bank with assets in seventy countries that was involved in an incredible variety of illegal activities, especially drug money laundering and terrorism. The bank was set up in a way to evade regulation by any one country; when that tactic did not work, it resorted to bribes, insider deals, and any other corrupt practice that might turn regulators into accomplices.

We didn't know all that when we started investigating BCCI. Along the way, I was on the receiving end of some serious pressure to turn down the heat, as the names of a number of prominent Democrats emerged as BCCI agents, facilitators, or dupes. As it turned out, we were able to unearth enough facts about the bank's crimes and evasions of U.S. law that our government, in conjunction with several others, felt compelled to shut the whole operation down.

From my experience on this investigation I learned two very important lessons that I will take to the White House with me.

The first is that our economic system really does depend on the reliability of the safeguards and institutions built up over the years to ensure transparency, arms-length transactions, the effectiveness of watchdogs, and other accountability measures. Capitalism has always relied on government to enforce these protections; without them, markets cannot function efficiently and private-sector players like investors cannot act with confidence. As president, I'll never forget that all the good economic policy in the world won't matter if our institutions, including the Security and Exchange Commission, aren't doing their job.

The second lesson I learned from BCCI is that it's all too easy for criminals and con artists to infiltrate the informal networks that link the business world to the political world—lobbyists, law firms, public-relations firms, consulting firms, and so forth. Shrewd manipulators, like the people running BCCI, are adept at using the good reputations of Americans to cover their bad intentions. That's why it's so important for elected officials and others holding positions of public trust to be especially vigilant about letting personal connections in the business world affect their decisions and their judgment. It's a very short step from cronyism to corruption. And I'm very concerned about the cronyism I see in almost every direction in the current administration.

Just as we need to restore confidence in markets, we also need to restore confidence in the government's economic and budget policies.

We should send a signal and set an example by simplifying the tax code to make sure that it puts the interests of all Americans ahead of special interests. We should close tax loopholes and be tough on corporate welfare. And we should reverse the renewed bad habits of the last few years and make a long-term commitment to restore a balanced budget—cutting wasteful spending so that we can free up private capital and investing in economic programs that actually work.

We can start by eliminating government subsidies that hurt our economy and punish our people. For example, offshore tax havens and tax shelters let corporations and executives evade an estimated twenty to forty billion dollars in taxes each year—taxes that must be made up by other taxpayers or by government borrowing. And these offshore havens rob us of more than tax dollars, for they are where renegade corporations flee from all responsibility to shareholders, employees, rules of fair play, and their own country. It's no accident that Enron had over 800 subsidiaries in countries with no taxes on income, profits, or capital gains. These included 692 in the Cayman Islands alone.

Taking on these abuses does not mean launching an attack on the legitimate overseas operations of American businesses. I believe in opening new markets, and I want American companies to compete and win everywhere they can. But brass-plate addresses with nothing behind the door but a fax machine are not legitimate enterprises.

This is not a small problem fiscally, economically, or ethically. Assets in offshore entities have risen from an estimated two hundred billion dollars in 1983 to roughly five trillion dollars today. And it is an issue that the president has said literally nothing about, and his administration has done literally nothing about. What does that silence convey to the vast majority of Americans who do pay taxes? In combination with the administration's drive to reduce taxes on the wealthiest Americans, it shouts loudly that the burden of paying for government in this country is being shifted from those most able to pay taxes to those least able to avoid taxes—the great American middle class.

In short, we need to stop cutting taxes on the privileged and begin reforming taxes by cracking down on corporate tax havens and loopholes and reviewing all our tax policies to restore the principles of fairness, simplicity, and efficiency that ought to underlie our system. I'd start by killing off corporate subsidies in the tax code and the federal budget. I know from experience that subsidy hunting is never in season in Washington and that it takes a sharp eye and a big gun to bag one, but as president, it's a challenge I'd accept.

When I came to the U.S. Senate in the 1980s, budget deficits were spiraling out of control and big national challenges were being ignored. We now see this pattern repeating itself. Then as now, it seemed to me that the first area in which we should restrain spending was in subsidies for private interests for which there was no compelling national, social, or economic rationale. But as the saying goes, you can't take the politics out of politics, and one senator's corporate subsidy is another senator's economic development program. So I went searching for one subsidy that pretty much everybody could understand was a boondoggle. That brought me to wool and mohair. This subsidy was created, believe it or not, in World War I to make sure that we had enough wool and mohair to make uniforms for the doughboys fighting in France and Belgium. After the war was won the doughboys returned home and we stopped using wool and mohair for uniforms—yet the wool and mohair subsidy lived on. The sheer absurdity of it made it a perfect example. So for

months I and a few of my colleagues went to the Senate floor again and again to call for a dignified funeral for this boondoggle, which we finally succeeded in killing off. Despite our efforts, however, it crawled right back into the federal budget in 2001. The joke in Washington, though it's not especially funny, is that the wool and mohair subsidy has provided the first definitive proof that immortal life is indeed possible.

Because special interests will stop at nothing to preserve such deals, it will take an extraordinary effort to eliminate pork that bloats the budget and hardens the arteries of our economy.

For that reason I've joined my friend and colleague John McCain in calling for a Corporate Subsidy Reform Commission modeled after the military base-closing commission. The idea is to ask a bipartisan group to draw up a list of corporate subsidies without any compelling economic or social justification and make Congress vote up or down on the whole package. Even if we miss a few big hogs in the budget, we expect the little piglets to add up. One recent defense bill, for example, included $250,000 to an Illinois company to research caffeinated chewing gum, $750,000 for grasshopper research in Alaska, $250,000 for a lettuce geneticist in California, and $64,000 for urban-pest research in Georgia. Gum, grasshoppers, lettuce, and roaches—these do not strike me as big defense priorities for America.

I don't believe and don't mean to suggest that these

questionable expenditures constitute a big part of the federal budget. But questioning them is a necessary step in attaining honest budgeting and fiscal responsibility. If we can't figure out how to defend taxpayers' dollars from private interests, we are unlikely to be able to determine how to invest them for good public purposes. And for my fellow Democrats, the challenge of budgetary vigilance is especially important. If we can't separate the sheep from the goats and instead treat all federal spending as equally justified, Republicans who say that investment is just a code word for spending have a point we can never refute. That's why I also think we should reimpose budget rules that limit annual increases in spending—rules recently suspended by congressional Republicans.

No member of either party can claim to advocate fairness in taxation if we continue to tolerate federal expenditures that shower tax dollars on beneficiaries that don't need them. The Fossil Energy Research and Development program provides more than four hundred million dollars to oil companies that can afford to pay for their own R&D. It even duplicates research they're already engaged in. And for 130 years the federal government has allowed companies to mine on publicly owned land for free and to buy these lands for ridiculous, below-market prices of five dollars an acre or less. That's corporate welfare. That's wasteful pork. That's unfair. If we simply required small, fair royalties and stopped giving away public lands we could save more than half a billion dollars over five years. That's worth doing.

Even as we cut waste and corporate welfare, we should emulate successful businesses by investing in projects that we know will make our people and our economy more productive in the future. Our first priority should be investments that both boost long-term economic growth and help us meet major national challenges. Energy independence is a great example of the sort of double-payoff strategy I'm talking about.

I'll address energy policy at greater length in a later chapter. For now I want to stress that a smart energy policy can also represent a smart economic policy. We can work toward energy independence—meaning independence not only from foreign energy sources but from environmentally damaging sources as well—in a way that calls on the best of America's creative and entrepreneurial spirit and improves both our quality of life and our national security.

In the 1960s President Kennedy challenged America to conquer space and land on the moon within a decade. It's time for a comparable Apollo Project approach to energy independence, with a focused effort that relies on public-private partnerships and creates millions of new jobs. To some extent, this Apollo Project would involve redeploying resources from the failed energy policies of the past and present. At present we spend $1.8 billion in subsidies to the oil and gas industries while investing only $24 million in federal venture capital for alternative energy sources. That's exactly the reverse of what our priorities should be. And the Bush administration seeks to accelerate this trend by moving heaven and most of all earth to expand oil drilling in some of our most sensitive environments. All this drilling won't produce significant quantities of oil for many years, so we will remain dependent on a global oil market whose prices are controlled—and often manipulated—by a handful of countries, lending permanent instability to our economy.

For Americans who work in engineering, design, and industry, the growth of wind, solar, and geothermal energy would spark a surge in production and jobs. And since developing new energy technologies requires research and pathbreaking applications, we can create thousands of high-paying new jobs in those areas as well. The machines of renewable energy will be made of steel, aluminum, and glass and will offer employment to machinists, manufacturers, distributors, and maintenance workers. Americans can take the lead, or we can let Germans or Japanese dominate this new industry.

Another double-payoff opportunity is in research and development of technologies we need for homeland security. In fact, these promise a triple payoff. The same technologies that help law-enforcement personnel find terrorists or react to terrorist attacks can also help us fight crime. And the same technologies that will help us detect, prevent, contain, and counter biological and chemical weapons can be applied in public health against epidemics like SARS. There's little incentive for private investors to enter this small but promising market where government may be the primary customer. So it makes abundant economic sense to create a publicly funded, privately managed venture-capital fund for such technologies.

But the investments we need in knowledge and research go well beyond health care. The Bush administration has embraced the most blatantly antiscience policies in a generation, stacking science review boards with ideologues, denying the need for new environmental technologies, trying to halt the astounding promise of stem cell research, and systematically underinvesting in basic science and research. I want to reverse those policies. And I will support stronger research efforts in the Department of Energy, NASA, and the National Science Foundation, along with a new commitment to breakthroughs in the next generation of innovation, such as nanotechnology and biotechnology research.

We can also produce an enormous economic payoff with relatively small but strategic investments in the quality of our workforce. America has the most talented and productive workers in the world, but that world keeps changing around them. For some, the effort to keep up can seem insurmountable, while others welcome job opportunities they could barely imagine a decade ago. It's long past time to turn workers who are threatened by the future into workers empowered by change. With state and local governments, higher educational institutions, and businesses and labor unions, the federal government needs to create a seamless system of worker training, based on locally identified needs for skills.

We should offer help to all workers at any stage of life who want to upgrade their skills, not just with scholarships for training programs but to offset the costs of résumé writing, job hunting, interviewing, and career research. If we are going to embrace a dynamic, high-turnover economy, we must also embrace worker-training programs that represent not just safety nets but trampolines to better jobs. But in addition to skills training, we also need to greatly increase access to higher education as part of any twenty-first-century economic strategy. If we are to maintain our edge in the information age, we must give every American the opportunity—not just in theory but in practice—to pursue four years of college. I am proposing a new College Opportunity Tax Credit that will make college more affordable by providing a tax credit on the first four thousand dollars of tuition, the typical cost of a public university. It will cover all of the first one thousand dollars in tuition costs and then half of the next three thousand dollars' worth. As I discuss in a later chapter, I also want to strike a new bargain with young people whereby we will cover the cost of four years at a public college in exchange for two years of national service to their country and their community.

The skills and knowledge to succeed in the global marketplace, however, will only benefit our people if we ensure real and fair opportunities in the global marketplace.

We should reenergize our trade policies to expand markets for our goods and services and revive worldwide economic growth while ensuring that workers and the enviroment are protected just as we protect our economic interests. I believe that with a level playing field, Americans can outcompete foreign companies every day of the week—and twice on Sunday. But we must enforce our trade agreements and our trade laws to ensure that level playing field. If I'm elected president, I will order an immediate top-to-bottom review of all trade agreements to determine and enforce compliance and will work to make observance of core labor standards and environmental protections an integral part of our trade expansion strategy.

Too often American companies are not on a level playing field. I believe we should stop giving incentives to companies that move overseas and instead give incentives to businesses that stay here at home. My new manufacturing job tax credit would relieve the payroll tax burden for a new employee any manufacturing company hires for the next two years. I also support incentives that would help ensure that Americans are ready to build the industries of the future. I have proposed giving subsidies and tax credits to companies that convert their plants to build the energy-efficient technology of the future. This will help make sure that the next generation of automobiles and appliances are built here in the USA.

And if we are going to ensure that there is a fair playing field for Americans, we have to crack down on our trading partners who are not playing fair and that includes countries, such as China, which have undermined our exports by manipulating currency.

The Bush administration has largely abandoned trade

expansion efforts and has never accepted the possibility that expanded markets can and should go hand in hand with progress on the environment and in labor conditions. The Clinton administration did not get very far in implementing its commitment to make a global economy work for all Americans by "expanding the winner's circle" of workers and communities prepared to succeed in the information age. But it was the right commitment to make, and it must be reestablished as national policy before opportunity here and abroad is allowed to shrink rather than expand.

Finally, we can get an enormous multiple payoff by investing in the technological infrastructure of the information age. As I said at the beginning of this chapter, the advent of a new economy has only paused, not stopped. There's a lot we can do to refresh the pool of innovation and entrepreneurial talent—of intellectual and human capital—that fed the Nineties boom and gave us a glimpse of a better way of life in which jobs pay well and satisfy the mind and spirit.

We can begin by making permanent the federal tax credit for research and development that helped supply much of the capital for the tech boom of the Nineties. That would send a strong signal that the country believes the new economy is something more than a temporary phenomenon.

The next step would be to expand high-speed Internet access to ensure that inner cities and rural areas become fully wired and to expand e-commerce. I've proposed a 10 percent tax credit for companies that set up broadband networks in inner cities, just as I earlier sponsored the e-rate law that finances the wiring of inner-city schools for the Internet. I would support any intelligent scheme for expanding broadband access that doesn't favor one technology over another and that would create a truly national platform for e-commerce and all the killer applications that will soon make the next stage of the digital economy self-sustaining. I've also helped craft and enact digital signature legislation that makes it possible to execute secure and private authorizations of e-commerce transactions, an essential step in expanding the digital economy and hence the national economy.

These issues are not just a recent sideline for me; they've been a big focus of my efforts in the Senate, in part because Massachusetts is, according to a Progressive Policy Institute study, the state most advanced toward a digital economy. I'm proud that *BusinessWeek* magazine named me one of its Digital Dozen, the twelve most tech-savvy members of Congress. I was the only Senate Democrat to make that list.

What I'm proudest of in this area is my involvement in sorting out the privacy issues associated with digital technology. If we don't quickly solve these problems, Americans will retreat from the Internet and the digital economy will truly crash. One of many of the things John McCain and I have done together in the Senate is to sponsor legislation on Internet privacy that would require Web sites to take steps to protect users' private information. It's an ap-

proach that tries to strike a balance between privacy concerns and the rights of Internet users to voluntarily provide
personal information to obtain the services they want.

✸

*Like many of you who are reading this book, I've been logging onto
the Internet and using e-mail for nearly a decade now. I've found it
to be an enormously useful tool, especially since I travel so frequently. It's helped me keep up with Senate business, with my staff,
with my constituents, and with the wider world of ideas and debate
that it's sometimes easy to miss in Washington. I read newspapers
and magazines online more than otherwise, and the Internet makes
it much more likely that I will be exposed to opinions different from
my own.*

*Most of all, e-mail makes it easier to stay in touch with my
family. My wife, Teresa, travels even more than I do in her capacity
as director of one of the country's largest foundations, one focused
heavily on environmental and health-care policy. We speak by phone
often when we are apart, but occasionally it's easier to get in touch
by e-mail. The same is true with my daughters and my stepsons.*

*I'm glad that all my kids are grown, however. When I log onto
e-mail and discover dozens of e-mails devoted to hawking sexual
aids; financial, real estate, and credit card come-ons; and plain,
graphic pornography, I know something is out of whack. This spam
is in danger of seriously undermining the most important Internet
application, and the ability of spammers to access Internet Web site
users means that spam is discouraging all the other applications as*

well. It's obvious that we need a way to can spam without abridging the First Amendment or inhibiting legitimate e-commerce, beginning with requiring an easily understandable and unequivocal subject-line that would at least alert e-mail users to the nature of unsolicited mail. We can't let the best thing that came out of the Nineties get strangled by bad content. Saving the Internet from hype and filth and making it a much more effective medium for learning, communicating, and legitimately and voluntarily buying and selling will be a major focus of the Kerry administration.

All these investments—in energy independence, homeland security, chronic-disease research, job skills, and new economy infrastructure—are designed to boost long-term economic growth while meeting other critical national challenges. The Bush administration is not especially interested in, much less committed to, any of these challenges. When his political advisers tell him to do so, the president may occasionally mention some of these areas or even co-opt Democratic proposals to actually do something about them, though usually on the cheap.

But the broader picture is simple, and its goals are unmistakable: The Bush administration's economic policies amount to nothing more than serial efforts to cut taxes for the wealthiest Americans and on unearned as opposed to earned income. These policies haven't worked, and won't work, to create jobs and growth. But they will unmistakably shift the tax burden from upper- to middle-income Americans while denying the country the financial resources it needs to begin to build its future.

We need an economic policy based on increasing our common wealth instead of squandering public resources to reward private privilege. As I've made plain, this will mean reversing ill-advised tax cuts for the wealthiest Americans. The super-rich did sensationally well under the Clinton-Gore policies that maintained progressive tax rates while encouraging economic growth. They'll do equally well under a Kerry administration—but not at the expense of other Americans or of future generations whose economic well-being is being mortgaged.

It's time to make a make a fundamental choice between two very different visions of the American economy. The Bush administration's vision is one in which Americans depend on the investment decisions of their wealthiest fellow-citizens for jobs, income, health care, skills, and technology. They will pay higher state and local taxes, higher college tuitions, higher health-care costs, higher training costs, and higher access fees for technology—all to work in insecure jobs at stagnant wages in a sluggish economy. I envision an America in which working families have a government that helps them find real opportunities, high-paying jobs, and better lifestyles; in which middle-class families are first in line for tax cuts; and in which our country's leaders know where to cut and where to invest to create economic growth while handling taxpayers' dollars fairly and efficiently.

I want a virtuous circle of prosperity with higher growth, higher incomes, greater wealth in every sector of our population, higher revenues, budget surpluses and low inflation, low unemployment, and lower interest rates. And I want to stop the current administration's slide towards slow growth, stagnant incomes, redistribution of wealth, sagging revenues, budget deficits, rising joblessness, and upward pressure on long-term interest rates.

There is absolutely no question that we can expand our common wealth. But we must first elect a leadership that understands how a modern global economy works and how we can work together to grow it and share its blessings.

The Challenge of Creating World-Class Schools

✷

Of the challenges I discuss in this book, education is as basic to America's future as any you can imagine. We are the richest society in the history of the world. We are the nation furthest advanced toward an information-age economy in which the knowledge and skills of our people are our most important labor *and* capital assets. We know that we need a rapidly expanding workforce of well-educated and well-trained individuals; they're more important to our economy than all our oil, minerals, or timber. We're already having to import human capital from all over the world. And we also know that the longstanding American aspirations of equal opportunity and upward mobility depend on an educational system that equips our people—all of our people—to occupy the high-wage jobs that brainpower can command.

It's rare to find an arena like education where determined public action can have so profound an impact on both our common destiny and our individual opportunities. And it's also rare to find an issue on which politics have so often stymied the adoption of the best solutions.

Certainly the task that we face is obvious. We once had the best public-education system in the world, much as we still have the best system of higher education. But the passage of our students from one system to the other tells the real tale. Today, nearly a third of all college freshmen require remedial classes in basic skills. In some parts of the country, the high school diploma has become not a testament to learning but simply a certificate of occasional attendance. A third of high school graduates are below-average readers. And despite some recent improvements, our high school students still perform below average on international science and math tests.

By and large, the kids who are being shortchanged by education below the college level are those who are most likely to have been shortchanged in other ways as well, with fewer family and community resources to support them as they grow up. We can talk endlessly about America's being a land of equal opportunity, but it's only talk if we are not willing to radically improve the performance of our schools, especially for those most in need of a step onto the ladder of upward mobility.

Why are we getting such varied results from our primary educational system? Why are we having to use our colleges and universities to teach fundamental skills?

Many individual factors contribute to the mixed performance of our public schools, especially in those inner-city and rural areas with the most disadvantaged school districts and students. There are physical infrastructure problems—schools that are falling apart. According to the National Center for Education Statistics, one in five of our schools is in poor physical condition, failing to meet building or safety codes and in urgent need of repair, renovation, or maintenance.

There are teacher shortages, especially in critical fields like science, math, and special education and in high-need schools in poorer areas. And in some places there are shortages in teacher quality as well. There's a special-education crisis around the country, with a rising percentage of students being classified as in need of special education. These kids are entitled to services while the federal government fails to bear its fair share of the spiraling cost. And there's a national early-childhood education crisis, with large differences in the extent to which kids are prepared to begin formal schooling and even larger differences in the help available to them to get ready to do so.

Complicating all these problems is the complexity of our system of federalism, which means that the roles of federal, state, and local governments in education vary enormously throughout the country. In particular, the reliance on property taxes to fund public education has resulted in large inequities in the resources available for schools.

Above all, there's a crisis of confidence among parents and taxpayers about the performance of traditional public schools and an increasingly heated controversy over alternatives such as charter public schools, magnet schools, and other innovations.

At the same time, many public schools *are* doing a great job, providing their students a first-rate education, which means we must be cautious about introducing education reforms that fix schools that aren't broke.

But the biggest problem, in my opinion, is a political debate on education that is all too often dominated by those who defend the status quo and by those who are prepared to abandon public schools entirely.

Certainly I am sympathetic to those whose instincts are to defend traditional public schools, their administrators, and, above all, their teachers against their many detractors.

It's true, as these defenders frequently argue, that schools often don't have the resources they need. Teachers are underpaid; in some parts of the country, grossly underpaid. It's true that we sometimes expect schools to deal with problems like student discipline, poor health, or emotional distress that are properly the responsibility of parents or society as a whole. And it's true that teachers have often been distracted from the hard work of teaching by the paperwork and testing regimes associated with various efforts to improve schools—efforts that often pile one on top of the other like layers of volcanic rock.

But sympathetic as I am to the defenders of our schools, I'm also sympathetic to the kids who are sometimes trapped in a failing school. As Hugh Price, president of the Urban League, said a few years ago: "We love our public schools, but we love our children even more." And however much we love and respect teachers and administrators, education policy should revolve around the needs of the children in the system.

The saddest commentary on American education—and for that matter, on the vitality of the longstanding American principle that teaching our children well is a common responsibility—is the boom in home schooling, which now represents the largest growth area in elementary and high school education. There always have been, and always will be, certain families who prefer home schooling as a matter of choice, whether for religious, pedagogical, or simply emotional reasons of their own. But there's little doubt that the current increase in home schooling is due in part to a negative reaction to the quality of some schools and their failure to nurture and develop the intellectual skills and moral qualities we expect. I feel about home schooling the way I feel about owning a firearm for self-protection—it's something every American should have the right to do but may not *have* to do if our public education system was realizing its potential.

I do not, however, believe that we should give up on public schools or give in to those who argue that public dollars should be strapped onto our children's backs to follow them into whatever private schools they can find. Down that path is the kind of balkanization—by money, race, religion, and region—that public education was designed to prevent in the first place.

Americans have always understood the connection between quality public education and equal opportunity. Here's what Horace Mann, a son of Massachusetts and the first superintendent of schools in the United States, said in 1830:

> *Our school buildings are little more than a skeleton of the structure a good schooling demands. Books are scarce, and there is a great divide between the amount of money one district in our cities spends on its young pupils and the amount of the public dollar committed to students in the outlying counties. Those who can are hiring private tutors and schooling the young in church schools and at home. As it stands in this era, our schools—those designed to educate our children in the new century—simply will endure no longer.*

> *I often quote Horace Mann's statement in speeches and in town meetings without at first telling the audience when it was written, because it sounds as if it could be a letter sent to the editor of almost any newspaper in the country on almost any day in the present. Maintaining the commitment to keep public schools public—in the broad sense of ensuring that they provide an equal foundation of knowledge and skills to every single child—is a hard but essential struggle. The common investment we make in public education is a big part of what makes our country a commonwealth in which we can all share in the fruits of wise investment.*

The federal government, of course, does not, and should not, run our public schools. But for four decades it has played a crucial role in seeing to it that poor school districts and disadvantaged kids get some assistance from the nation as a whole. The programmatic name for this assistance is the Elementary and Secondary Education Act (ESEA), established during the Great Society at a time when we were acutely aware that many states and school districts had systematically neglected the educational needs of African-Americans specifically and poor families generally.

Over time this program, like many federal programs, became something of an end in itself. Because Congress operates by spreading money around to as many states and districts as possible, ESEA ultimately became less focused on the truly needy schools and students. And since there was much more of a consensus about the content of good educational practices than about the measures of results they should obtain, federal education policy is often focused on inputs—on micromanaging how schools operated—rather than on outcomes, the skills and knowledge we want our children to take with them from the classroom. The stress on inputs served to multiply the bureaucracy and paperwork that overwhelms local school administrators and teachers alike.

In the late 1990s education reformers from both parties and from every part of the country started to come together to push for an overhaul of this critical federal education program. I made a speech at Northeastern University in Boston

in 1998 that was one voice in this chorus—a fairly provoca-
tive voice at that, since I was fed up with the pointless education debate in Washington.

I later introduced my own comprehensive education
reform bill in the Senate. Then, when momentum built behind a similar, bipartisan proposal, I sponsored an effort for
change. In 2001 President Bush endorsed what had been a
centrist Democratic bill; the result was the No Child Left
Behind Act. The law was not perfect and some of its reforms need significant changes. But particularly in a time
when the administration and both Houses of Congress
were Republican, it held the promise of good bipartisan reform. The federal government would now begin rewarding
success in schools serving disadvantaged kids. More money
would be aimed at schools and children truly in need.
School districts performing poorly would be pushed to innovate, to provide parents with choice within the public
schools, including charter public schools. Failing schools
would be given resources and technical assistance and if after they still weren't performing well, they would be re-
organized. Teachers would be given a set period of time
to become proficient in the subjects they teach.

Its key idea was a new bargain: accountability for results in exchange for the new resources necessary to achieve
those results. The president embraced that bargain and took
a lot of personal credit for the legislation. That wasn't surprising, since No Child Left Behind was his one significant
bipartisan initiative and the one part of his domestic agenda

that was neither an empty shell nor an effort to turn back the clock.

But before the ink was even dry on the act, the president abandoned the new bargain by denying states and school districts the promised federal resources. Like virtually every other item on the domestic agenda, education reform has been sacrificed to the overriding administration priority of cutting taxes on high earners in a budget already flooded with red ink. Congress has forced some new spending on the administration, but it's been a constant struggle even to keep our investment in public schools at current levels. Moreover, the funding to implement the initiative competes with other educational requirements, such as money to cover the federal share of special-education costs. And it comes at a time when, in part because of Bush's economic choices, states are forced to cut back. As a result, we now have states, school districts, schools, teachers, and students all held to higher standards without the foundation to achieve them, and in many cases set up for failure—set up, in fact, to be left behind as the intellectual demands on the U.S. workforce continue to increase over the next generation.

Moreover, the abandonment of the grand bargain of more resources and flexibility in exchange for results sets up education reform for failure—a failure that could well sour the American people as a whole on the possibility of substantive positive changes in our public schools.

There's no question that there are those in the Administration—and, even more so, in the Republican Party—who would applaud this development. Some conservatives openly oppose education reform because they don't consider public schools worth saving. They prefer subsidies to go to private schools that have no accountability for achieving specific educational results, letting market forces dictate what knowledge and skills we want our children to possess. Many Republicans are absolutists when it comes to moral standards of right and wrong but, ironically, are relativists when it comes to educational standards of knowledge and ignorance.

Without presidential leadership, the latest wave of education reform will quickly unravel, leading us right back to the old stalemate between those who resist reform of public schools and those who want to replace them with a publicly subsidized network of private schools.

My agenda for public education rejects both of those narrow approaches.

If I'm elected president, I will make lifting the performance of public schools and giving them the tools and flexibility to succeed the top educational priority of my administration.

There are other steps I will take to make all our public schools world-class institutions, the foundation of a world-class economy and society.

First, we need to place more emphasis on teaching and less on bureaucracy. Look at most school boards in this country and you will see a classic industrial-age bureaucracy seeking to own and operate every aspect of public education and to micromanage the activities of everyone working in the schools. In urban and suburban districts, school boards are often large, unwieldy agencies full of factions representing various constituencies that combine to make oversight and leadership a challenge. And for all of the power of school boards few of them impose real accountability for results on the schools they oversee.

In other words, many public schools are governed by a system that neither provides effective leadership at the top nor accepts leadership in individual schools or classrooms. The result is that no one is really held responsible for the education of our kids. The managers of our public schools, the superintendents and principals, are often left to be scapegoats for complaints by parents and taxpayers. The average term of a public school superintendent in this country is three years—hardly enough time to change the culture of a school district, build lasting relationships, or establish continuity.

We need to give public institutions more freedom from micromanagement in exchange for strict accountability for achieving tangible improvements in the knowledge and skills of our children.

You have to observe a good charter school in action to appreciate the revolutionary nature of what too often sounds like an academic concept. I've seen one in Lawrence, Massachusetts, in the Community Day Charter School. This school, with Kindergarten through

eighth grade, has a student body that is 80 percent Hispanic, more than two-thirds of whom are poor enough to qualify for free or subsidized school lunches. Community Day has no particular gimmicks and no particular advantages over other schools beyond flexibility keyed to results and a lot of determination. Every student is given a personal education goal and an attainment strategy, based on his or her strengths. And the concept works. In the 2001–02 school year, Community Day students had the best statewide test scores in Lawrence. In grades 4–8, the kids ranked in the top 15 percent of the state. Such impressive results are not uncommon for Massachusetts charter schools: Two thirds of charter school classes had statewide test scores that topped their school districts. I often think about the fact that Community Day has a waiting list of over five hundred kids. We need to empower every school in the public school system to apply the best practices from schools across the country.

I believe it's time to stop viewing innovative approaches as anomalies or threats to traditional public schools and begin seeing them as part of the future of public education. Our goal should be to empower every public school to establish clear expectations and accountability and be allowed much more freedom to innovate in how results are achieved.

Many have argued for reform through the public financing of vouchers for private schools, but I believe this is pushing the country in the wrong direction. Vouchers allocate resources not among competing public schools but out of the system entirely. Private schools accepting vouchers do not agree to accept kids on an equal basis and also do not guarantee that the voucher will cover the cost of the education. And most objectionally, voucher schemes do not hold private schools accountable in any way for the educational results they achieve—or do not achieve.

Confusing public school choice and innovation isn't just a matter of comparing apples and oranges—it's comparing apples and worms. There's nothing that's good about a voucher system—parental choice, competition, and the ability to provide innovative instruction—that can't also be achieved by public education. But the kind of public schools we ought to have *can* avoid what's bad about vouchers: the inequality, the lack of accountability, and the gradual erosion of our sense of commonwealth.

The second step in my program to improve schools is to reinvent the way we recruit, train, and reward the most important adults in our educational system, our teachers.

There's no question that elementary and secondary teachers have one of the toughest, not to mention one of the most critical, jobs in America. And for all the lip service we pay to them, there's no question we pay them too little money and grant them too little genuine respect for what they contribute to their communities and their country. That's not to say that there aren't variations in teacher ability as well as in teacher pay. And part of the price of years of indifference and neglect in this area is that we do not attract as many of the best students as we ought to.

The urgency of this issue is compounded by a teacher shortage. We need an estimated two million new teachers over the next decade. The need is most acute in the schools—those serving disadvantaged kids—and the subjects—especially math, science, and special education—that are most critical to the goal of leaving no child behind. Since most school systems will continue to try to reduce class sizes, especially in elementary schools, the teacher shortage could soon grow much worse.

A clear priority is to begin attracting top-notch college students to teaching, particularly in difficult urban and rural settings. Obviously, higher pay for all teachers would help. We must also invest in improving teacher quality. In fact, if you look at the parts of our educational system that do attract high-quality college graduates, it becomes obvious that salary is only one relevant factor and not always the most important.

We have to treat teachers like the professionals they are—empowering them to run their own classrooms and empowering them to play more leadership roles in school.

While breaking down the current barriers to entry into the teaching profession does mean allowing more liberal certification procedures, it shouldn't mean that candidates receive less instruction in how to teach. Indeed, a more open certification process should go hand in hand with a greater emphasis on classroom experience and peer training. We need to adopt the American Federation of Teachers' proposal for greater mentoring and induction training for new teachers as part of a broader effort to encourage continuing professional development for teachers. This approach would also help liberate school principals to hire and retain teachers based on what they know and what they can do instead of a one-time certification before they enter the classroom.

Opening the doors to the teaching profession means more, however, than simply recruiting top-notch college graduates. It also means recruiting midcareer talent—men and women who have demonstrated their mettle in other fields and who now want to learn how to teach in order to apply their experience to the classroom. We have a Peace Corps that sends Americans around the world to bring entrepreneurial and technical skills to bear on the problems of other countries. We have an AmeriCorps that deploys young people to help meet the challenges of underserved American communities. We need a similar call to service—and an equivalent mobilization of talent—to meet the crucial educational challenge we face during the next decade. We need to create a Twenty-first Century Teaching Corps of midcareer professionals loaned and paid for by the corporate sector, which would recognize the huge stake that business has in the education of the next generation of executives, technicians, managers, and workers.

But all our efforts to attract new talent to teaching and other educational occupations will fall short if we don't also revisit the system of evaluating and rewarding teachers so that there is recognition of how successfully they have done their jobs. We need to replace established procedures of teacher tenure with fair dismissal policies, like we passed in Massachusetts, that discourage political hirings and firings and cronyism. No teacher should fear losing his or her job because of front-office politics or favoritism. But no teacher should have a lock on a job regardless of performance, and it should not take tens of thousands of dollars and years in courtrooms to dismiss an ineffective teacher.

There are other specific steps we can take to renew education in this country. We should offer knowledge- and skills-based supplemental pay for teachers who have mastered particular skills that will contribute to student achievement, such as subject-matter mastery. And we should also offer supplemental pay to teachers who choose to serve in hard-to-fill subject areas, and disciplines where there are demonstrated shortages and in hard-to-staff schools like those serving disadvantaged students.

We cannot expect to make schools accountable for their actual performance unless we are willing to make needed investments in schools and hold those who actually work in schools accountable as well. If we do so, we can finally begin to break the vicious cycle of taxpayers' refusing to grant more resources to schools that aren't succeeding and schools' falling short of the resources to get the job done.

★

One of the things that worries me most about the future of American education is the erosion I see in the belief that public schools are a common responsibility of our citizenry, not just a matter of concern for parents with school-age kids. This growing disregard for the common commitment to education is dangerous for several reasons.

As a country, we are experiencing a large increase in the number of families without school-age kids. That's happening in part because many married couples are delaying childbearing until much later in their lives. The biggest reason is simply that empty-nesters—married couples whose children are grown—are becoming a much larger part of the population every year, a result of the combination of longer lifespan and the sheer demographic weight of the baby-boom generation.

In addition, higher birthrates among African Americans and Hispanics means that their children make up an ever-higher percentage of the school-age population. White baby boomers face a real, seductive temptation to resist investments in public schools because only the futures of somebody else's children—generationally and ethnically—are at stake.

It's the same temptation our country faced and overcame a century ago when the public schools in most major cities were overwhelmed by immigrants—Italians, Poles, Irish, Jews, Czechs, Slovaks, Croatians, Greeks, Portuguese, Russians, and Ukrainians, among others. As that generation of Americans reaffirmed, the purpose of public schools is not to relieve parents of the cost of education but to relieve the nation of the cost of ignorance, intolerance, and ethnic isolation.

✳

The third big step we need to take in education is to pay more attention to what happens before kids enter school and what they do after the bell rings each day to send them to homes that are too often empty.

Early childhood development has been not simply an interest but a real passion for me and my wife, Teresa, for years. When you read about the breakthrough findings in the world of science you learn just how crucial the early years of life are in shaping every future learning and development opportunity. But the sad irony is that as we begin to understand the critical role of early childhood development, it has become harder and harder for parents to spend time with their kids. As a country, we are engaged in a dangerous experiment to see how little attention our children can actually be paid in the early stages of their development. I think we need to reduce the risk this situation poses and at least give parents more options and children more help.

We should expand the child tax credit as quickly as possible. At the same time, we should begin to catch up with the rest of the world by providing paid parental leave for parents with infants. These two initiatives together would make it much easier for one parent to stay at home during the most critical phases of early childhood.

We also have to expand prekindergarten education and other similar platforms for cognitive learning. I'm proud to have sponsored an effort that helps families by providing funding to increase and coordinate early childhood development initiatives. But this is only a start.

It's equally important that we see to it that kids have something useful to do after school. Every day five million American kids are home alone or on the streets between the hours of 2 and 7 P.M. In most cases, we consider ourselves lucky when the television can become their caretaker, because otherwise, too many kids might use this time to conceive a child, do drugs, or commit violent crimes. I've sponsored legislation in the Senate to encourage schools to keep their doors open after regular school hours for programs that provide recreational and educational opportunities.

Today's kids are especially vulnerable because we are in the middle of a huge transition in how families—or at least many families—are organized. The emancipation of women to go into the workplace and the advent of two-earner families are not just economic or social trends; they represent enormous changes in social structure that will take decades to work themselves out thoroughly. While there are thousands of self-help books on the subject, there's no guaranteed successful approach to raising kids and working full time. We need to do everything we can to support parents in this effort.

I know from personal experience how complicated this task can be. In 1982 my first wife and I separated. When I was elected to the U.S. Senate in 1984, she stayed in Boston with our children while I traveled to Washington. Trying to do honor to my duties as a father as well as my duties to the people of Massachusetts, I would sometimes sneak away from my staff and put in a call to my daughters to check on their homework or just talk to them about the ups and downs of their day.

On Thursdays or Fridays I'd fly back to Boston as soon as Senate business was finished and would sometimes get back just in time to catch the final minutes of Vanessa's soccer games. When they'd end, I'd usually run onto the field to give her a hug and congratulate her on her effort, and it always hurt that I had missed part of the game. (Sometimes, she didn't return the hug, and it was only years later, while watching a televised interview with her, did I learn the truth: She was embarrassed by the fluorescent orange hunting cap I occasionally wore to her games in the late fall.)

Like most parents, I made some mistakes. But I learned a lesson during those years that everybody in Washington ought to learn about the challenge most American families face as they try to balance work and parenting. Some people mocked Al Gore for making this issue a priority in 2000, as though it were a trifling concern affecting only spoiled baby boomers working too many hours and living too far from their jobs. But it's a very real problem for most families, and while government cannot solve it, all our policies should reflect an understanding of how important it is to support parents who leave one job each afternoon to return home to the most important job in America.

To be truly committed to fostering childhood development means recognizing that it is inevitably a complex phenomenon that involves a combination of good health care, sound parenting, early and effective cognitive development, and strong school-based programs to make sure kids get the right kind of education after school as well. It often takes the efforts of an extended family to effectively raise kids. Child-rearing begins with the nuclear family, but it always has and always will depend on the active involvement of grandparents, aunts and uncles, neighbors, friends, and sometimes the broader community. As a country, we should not only honor but support in every way possible the role of the immediate family in raising kids and in transmitting the values of our civilization. But especially when there's no family present or when family fails, we should be prepared to act as catchers in the rye to ensure that kids are not abandoned.

We should also support families by honestly acknowledging that our schools, for better or worse, convey values to the students under their care for twelve, thirteen, fourteen, or more years. Pretending they don't, or trying to promote a values-free education out of fear of controversy or lawsuits, only sends its own sad message of watery convictions and weak character. When we refuse to teach our children values for fear of offending someone, we empower others, such as gangs, to devalue the things we care most about.

We need curriculums that give our children both rules and role models so that we're not teaching them, for example, that violence is wrong only after they've seen it directly affect their classmates.

By rules for schools, I mean codes of discipline that carry consequences. Every school should write its own discipline code, ask every parent and child to sign it, and enforce its terms. When students become a threat to others or when they keep others from learning, they shouldn't be kept in the classroom. We must insist on separating disruptive students from their peers and provide resources for alternative ways of educating them, such as second-chance schools with tough rules and psychological help for at-risk kids.

The best character education we can offer our children is to inculcate a spirit of mutual respect and reciprocal obligation in them. The best way to do that is to encourage a commitment to service. Every high school in the country should make it a graduation requirement that students spend time in some form of community service—after school, on weekends, or during the summers. And in pursuance of the principle that every student should both learn and serve, we should change the college work-study program that currently employs hundreds of thousands of college students in campus-based jobs so they can work as mentors to at-risk kids in our public schools.

Linking service to educational opportunity can't stop at the classroom door. We also need service opportunities for the young who have dropped out of school or don't have the resources to continue their educations. That's the principle behind one of my favorite civic initiatives, the YouthBuild program.

★

Back in 1978, a woman named Dorothy Stoneman, along with a group of local teenagers, set out to restore a tenement house in Harlem to serve as a shelter for homeless people. They wound up building much more than a house, for it proved to be the first step toward what we know today as the YouthBuild initiative, a public-private partnership that employs at-risk youth in the construction of new housing for low-income and homeless people at two hundred sites in forty-four states. I've been involved with YouthBuild as an occasional participant and a regular advocate for about ten years, and every time I visit one of its work sites my faith in the regenerative power of service is renewed. During the past ten years, twenty-five thousand young people have built over ten thousand units of low-income housing—in the aggregate, a small city of big dreams realized.

YouthBuild is open to unemployed young people between the ages of sixteen and twenty-four. Most of them have been in some kind of trouble. Some of them are still struggling to stay in school, and they alternate weeks on the job site with weeks in the classroom. They are turning their own lives around as they turn around neighborhoods by building new housing. While they work on carpentry or masonry they also work toward a diploma, a certificate in a useful construction skill, or a job. YouthBuild kids take weekly classes in how to manage time effectively, develop a career plan, and handle job interviews. At work sites, they get close supervision and training from high-quality instructors, often union journeymen.

During the past decade YouthBuild has operated in partnership with the AmeriCorps national service program, the domestic Peace Corps begun under President Clinton to give young people the chance to earn college scholarships in exchange for a year or two *of service to the community in a broad range of critical tasks, from conservation to crime prevention to literacy and home health care. That partnership means that many YouthBuild participants are now able to go on to college.*

I'm sure many YouthBuild participants and alumni were as gratified as I was when President Bush made national service a central theme of his State of the Union Address in 2002, calling, among other things, for a doubling of the size of AmeriCorps. I'm sure they were equally disappointed when this pledge was abandoned, and Congressional Republicans instead cut AmeriCorps in half, actually shutting the program down for a while despite a record number of applications from young people answering the president's call.

If we as a country cannot see the value of initiatives like YouthBuild—a value measured not just in the dollars and cents of new housing stock and higher property values but in lives saved, crimes uncommitted, and prison cells unoccupied—we are incapable of intelligently allocating resources at all. If I'm president, we will look high and low—and work day and night—to develop, find, and help sustain civic bargains and moral bonanzas like Youth-Build.

Of course, it's impossible for me to describe in a single chapter or even an entire book all we need to do to build world-class schools and make them part of a lifelong learning system that equips Americans for the high-wage jobs and more creative occupations opened up by our country's scientific and technological preeminence. Some reforms are best left to state and local governments or civic partnerships, although our chief executive should be aware of them and the federal government supportive of them with an appropriate level of resources and clear expectations for their use.

As I write this book, Congress is taking a fresh look at special education, and I hope we can finally break the stalemate between those who argue the federal government should pick up its fair share of the heavy costs involved in it and those who say we should first reform the program to ensure that the right kids are getting the right kind of help. I think both should be considered priorities. We've done a good job over the last decade or so in making sure that children with disabilities get access to special services, but we've been less successful in making special education accountable for real-life results. We need the same sort of accountability push in special education that No Child Left Behind offers—if we fund and implement it—to the education of disadvantaged kids generally.

I haven't talked much about higher education here. That's because I believe our system is basically sound. Our main challenge in this area is to make sure that every American child has the chance to go to college, and opening the doors of college would be an important priority in my administration. I'm strongly in favor of protecting diversity and outreach programs in our colleges and universities from attacks by right-wing ideologues. And I strongly favor enhancing the value of the Pell grants that help so many poor and minority kids afford college.

The 1990s brought a variety of new tax incentives to

help families pay for college, including the HOPE Scholarship and tax preferences for college savings. I think it's time to ensure that all Americans can afford four years of college. I've proposed a College Opportunity Tax Credit that will help make four years of college as universal as a high school education is today. And my Service for College Initiative will pay for college for students who give two years of service to their country.

In every area of education policy a Kerry administration will understand the value of world-class schools not as an end in itself but as the means by which our country prepares its citizenry for a dramatically evolving national and world economy, one in which brainpower will be critical in almost every occupation, even those now thought of as unskilled. We will focus on results, not just inputs, and will consult the stakeholders in our educational system without letting any single interest or combinations of interest dictate policy.

When it comes to their living up to their rhetoric and keeping their promises, it's time to treat political leaders the way we treat schools and teachers in a system of accountability. Let's accept a charter as a nation to achieve clear results in the skills and knowledge of our people. And when our promises to our children are broken—as they are today—that means it's time for new leadership.

The Challenge of Creating a Modern Health-Care System

*

Ever since the 1990s, when the last comprehensive health initiative crashed and burned, the country has had a hard time regaining any sort of perspective on our health-care system. A few basic truths about that system, however, remain obvious.

For those who can afford it we have the best health-care system in the world. But we are the only major industrialized country that does not guarantee every citizen, regardless of income, access to affordable health care. The problem of obtaining that care is especially acute for middle-class families who do not qualify for public-assistance programs.

While we have the best health-care professionals, our system is constantly wracked by battles among shifting coalitions of those professionals, hospitals, businesses, and other big purchasers of health-care packages, insurance companies, and lawyers—battles that increase costs and endanger quality.

We have the best health-research facilities, again by a large margin. But our system encourages expenditures on the treatment of chronic diseases once they become acute, rather than preventing, managing, or curing them. We expect miracles from our great medical research centers while often undermining their efforts by how we allocate our resources.

We lead the world in pharmaceutical research and development but don't do enough to make sure the products are affordable. Their skyrocketing cost and the failure of some insurance plans like Medicare even to cover them have created an economic crisis for too many families of which a member suffers from chronic illnesses requiring expensive drugs—prescriptions many cannot afford to pay for.

And there's another truth that makes the current health-care debate in this country especially urgent: Some of the bad features of our health-care system are getting worse and fast. Health-care inflation, which subsided during the mid- to late 1990s, has now returned with a vengeance. Monthly insurance premiums went up by double digits in 2002 and 2003—at eight times the general increase in the cost of living. At current rates total annual national spending on health care is expected to reach $2.8 trillion by the end of this decade—double the amount we spent at its beginning.

The number of Americans with no health insurance at all remains scandalously high and could soon reach even higher levels, in part because rising premiums are once again inhibiting small businesses from providing coverage for their employees and in part because fiscally strapped states are tightening eligibility for public programs like Medicaid and the Children's Insurance Program. This problem is especially alarming because of the long-term medical, social, economic, and moral costs associated with neglecting health care for children.

And there are signs that the quality of health care all Americans receive is in danger of being compromised by all the financial and institutional pressures—all the bureaucracy and paperwork—that now burden health-care professionals. The number of medical errors seems to be increasing even as the treatments and technologies to make good medicine easier become more widely available.

Finally, millions of elderly Americans live in fear that they will spend their remaining years in a nursing home because we have no national strategy for long-term care.

There are four ways we can deal with these problems as a country.

First, we can confront the issues of cost, access, and quality in a piecemeal way, much as we did during most of the last decade. Incremental reform is a well-intentioned approach, but it does not account for the way in which different problems in our health-care system are interrelated.

Second, we could try to overwhelm the problems with a massive expansion of the federal government's role in health care, as some have proposed.

Third, we could choose not to institute any reforms at

all, distorting the medical profession's motto of "First, do no harm" into "Do nothing." That is essentially the position of the Bush administration. Granted, the administration takes positions on health-care issues now and then, typically when its polls show that it must or when Democrats introduce a proposal that it seeks to counter or co-opt. The president came up with a Patients' Bill of Rights alternative just in time to head off a bipartisan congressional proposal and block the passage of any bill at all. And occasionally the president or his party makes noises about providing tax credits so that the uninsured can buy insurance—even though the credits they discuss are far too small to cover the actual premiums and no plan is offered of how to hold down costs or increase the buying power of consumers.

Health care is an area in which presidential leadership is indispensable, if only because so many powerful special interests have a stake in almost every aspect of health policy. They are vigilant and deeply entrenched in Washington, and, as the infamous Harry and Louise ads of 1994 demonstrated, they can mobilize at the drop of a hat. Making any sort of inroads on health reform will require a president who goes to the Oval Office every morning resolved to accomplish fundamental change—a president with a vision of a modernized health-care system that can delivery quality, affordable health care to every family. That's the fourth alternative, and that's my resolve.

★

Health-care policy is one area where I have something of a built-in kitchen cabinet—quite literally in my own kitchen. I'm very proud that my daughter Vanessa is at Harvard Medical School training to be a doctor. My late father-in-law was a physician in East Africa, one of the toughest but most rewarding places in the world to practice medicine. And partly because of her upbringing, my wife, Teresa, has devoted a lot of her energy, attention, and resources as chairman of the Heinz Family Philanthropies to developing health-care strategies and solutions, especially for women's health, environmental health, prescription-drug coverage for seniors, and affordable health insurance for all Americans.

So if as president I ever forgot my promises about health care for even a day, I would be reminded of them by two of the most important—and the most persuasive—people in my life.

I learned a personal lesson in the importance of persistence in obtaining quality health care just a few years ago when I became involved, along with several other members of the Massachusetts congressional delegation, in a nurses' strike at a hospital in the town of Brockton. The strike was compelling to me because these nurses' demands were primarily focused not on their own wages or benefits or their own well-being, but on the quality of care they felt they owed to their patients. They were concerned about mandatory overtime work that often left them too tired to do their jobs well, and they were concerned about rotation systems that sometimes required nurses to work in units requiring specialized training that they had not received. The strike, called by the Massachusetts Nurses Association as the collective bargaining agent for the 450 nurses at Brockton Hospital, went on for ninety-two days, from May 25 to August 24, 2001.

Concerned that the stalemate might never be broken, I made a few phone calls to people on both sides of the strike, concluded there might be grounds for an agreement, presented a draft proposal to the nurses' union that might serve as the basis for a breakthrough, and offered my services to both sides as a mediator. For fourteen hours I shuttled back and forth between the hospital's negotiators and the nurses' negotiators. At 11 P.M., when everyone was exhausted, I was able to walk into the room with the nurses' team and announce: "I think we have reached an agreement."

Indeed we had—and the nurses were able to achieve their main objectives: convincing the hospital to hire more staff and reduce mandatory overtime and inappropriate rotations.

I tell this story not to take credit for ending the Brockton strike—the two parties involved did that—but as token of the fact that I understand the complexity of health-care issues, the high emotions involved in resolving them, and the need for patience and tenacity in forging a consensus. I know I have those qualities and will use them to the fullest possible extent in forging a national solution to our health-care crisis.

That fourth option I offer is a proposal that breaks new ground in the health-insurance debate by simultaneously addressing three challenges that are central to modernizing our health-care system: first and foremost, bringing costs under control; offering access to affordable coverage, with plenty of choices, to every American; and guaranteeing that every child in America will have health insurance coverage.

My plan builds on and strengthens the current public/private system of health care and at the same time simplifies it. I don't want to increase the bureaucracy in our health-care system; I want to slash it. I don't want to impair research and medical advancement in the private sector; I want to advance it. And I definitely don't want to put Americans in some sort of one-size-fits-all health-care program; I want to give them more affordable options and greater choices. My plan, therefore, strengthens what works now, rewards what's right, helps those who most deserve it, cracks down on those skimming the system for windfall profits, and ensures that cutting-edge technologies are used to make Americans healthier and health care more affordable.

It starts with an effort to deal with health-care costs, because if we don't bring them under control, everything else we try to do will become far more expensive than it ought to be. Moreover, spiraling health-care costs afflict everybody in the system. They widen the gap between what the uninsured can afford and the health insurance they need, while at the same time forcing families who do have insurance to pay increasing premiums, deductibles, and co-payments. High costs are becoming an ever greater problem for employers, both the small businesses who are near the line where they must decide whether to provide health insurance for their employees and the larger businesses that may restrict the coverage they do provide or limit their share of the premiums. High costs are also wreaking havoc on state budgets, threatening coverage for poor families and kids, forcing increases in taxes and fees, and crowding out other priorities like education and law enforcement.

We can, however, hold these costs in line without relying on government price controls or other outmoded and counterproductive approaches. We can do so first by focusing on catastrophic health costs. Claims in excess of fifty thousand dollars represent 20 percent of medical expenses for private insurers yet less than ½ of 1 percent of all claims. They not only boost premiums and bankrupt people with little or no insurance; they also inhibit employers from covering employees. I propose a new approach in which the federal government will cover 75 percent of the cost of catastrophic claims (those over fifty thousand dollars) for companies that agree to three conditions: provide affordable coverage for all their workers, pass on premium savings to their employees, and put in place preventive care and programs to promote better overall health. Throughout the system, I believe we must emphasize disease prevention and health promotion. This plan can reduce average premiums by nearly 10 percent. It can also help reverse the erosion of employer-based coverage and the trend that's making it harder for new employees to get coverage to begin with.

Most important, this premium rebate plan will strongly encourage employers to buy insurance that focuses on prevention, management of chronic diseases, and, in general, the long-term health of patients rather than simply the treatment of conditions. This is the cutting edge of modern medicine, and it will help keep people healthier while significantly reducing costs in the long run.

In other words, I want to make existing employer-based insurance more expansive in coverage, less expensive to both employers and employees, and more modern in its approach to patients' health. And I want to accomplish that in a way that does not upset the basic structure of employer-sponsored insurance.

Next, I would use market forces and the purchasing power of the federal government to slow down the spiraling prices of prescription drugs. Today those prices are rising on average by about 20 percent each year. Government-imposed price controls are not a feasible option because they might lead to products' being taken off the market and could dangerously interfere with private-sector research into groundbreaking and lifesaving medications. Instead, I'd start by using the simple power of transparency to hold down prices. Pharmacy-benefit managers currently oversee drug benefits for over two hundred million Americans. They often get rebates from drug companies that they don't pass on to consumers. With disclosure of the incentives benefit managers pocket, big purchasers like the federal government will be able to push them to cut prices for consumers, and the whole market will benefit. I also believe drug companies themselves, as a matter of honesty, should disclose the amount of money they spend influencing doctors to prescribe their brands, an expenditure that should be put to better use.

Speaking of drug companies, I support their right to make profits on groundbreaking drugs during the period for which they hold a patent. But when those patents expire, consumers should be able to benefit from the option of purchasing lower-cost generic drugs. There are now loopholes in patent law that keep cheaper alternatives off the market for years, even decades. I propose to plug those loopholes and create competitive markets that will significantly keep prices in check by an estimated $60 billion over the next decade. That will not only make a prescription-drug benefit under Medicare more affordable but will also produce federal government savings that could help pay for it.

Another step I'd take on prescription drugs is to let states negotiate better drug prices for Americans without prescription drug coverage who today pay up to 50 percent markups compared with bulk purchasers. I would reverse the position of the Bush administration and side with states that are trying to extend the drug discounts they negotiate through the Medicaid program to other parts of the population.

Medical malpractice is another area in which my plan would control costs. This is a subject that some Democrats have shied away from, fearing that it might offend trial lawyers, an important source of campaign dollars for many Democratic candidates. I don't, however, want to do anything that would prevent victims of medical malpractice from recovering justice and compensation for their suffering. That's why I oppose capping damages in medical malpractice cases, as the Bush administration and its congressional allies have proposed. Such caps would affect precisely those victims of malpractice that have valid, sometimes heartbreakingly compelling claims. Instead, I want to put an end to the kind of frivolous malpractice suits that are too often filed in the hopes of extorting a settlement. My plan would assure that an individual who brings a medical malpractice action has had a qualified tribunal including a lawyer and a medical specialist determine that a reasonable claim exists. It would impose sanctions on lawyers who initiate lawsuits not based on any legitimate legal cause, it would encourage states to require nonbinding mediation before lawsuits proceed on medical liability claims, and it would raise the bar for punitive damages in malpractice cases unless intentional misconduct, gross negligence, or reckless indifference to life is proved.

We can also reduce medical costs by encouraging the use of new information technologies to cut red tape and bureaucracy while reducing medical errors—saving both dollars and lives in the process.

One-quarter of the money Americans spend on health care each year—about $350 billion—goes to nonmedical costs, with much of that devoted to preparing, submitting, calculating, paying, and collecting medical bills. No other industry is so inefficient in this regard. Many banks, for example, have cut their costs to less than a penny per transaction using computers and other technology. Yet the simple transactional costs necessary to process a single health-care visit can cost as much as twenty-five dollars.

I want to use all the levers of the federal government to encourage a technology revolution in American health care. My immediate goals will be to ensure that, by the end of my service as president, all Americans will have secure, private electronic medical records, which will drastically reduce the need for redundant medical tests, and to require the federal government—and private insurers doing business with the federal government—to adopt the modern, computerized methods for handling health-care transactions that other industries use. These reforms have already begun to be applied in the veterans' health system, which I watch very closely. It used to cost the Veterans Administration nine dollars to pull an entire medical record for a single patient. With computerized records, it now costs nothing at all. I believe we can cut administrative expenses in half in our health-care system, saving $175 billion a year, if we launch this technology revolution immediately.

At the same time, new technologies can help us radically reduce medical errors and encourage the monitoring of medical outcomes so that we can measure the health of our people, not just how often they are treated. A recent Institute of Medicine study found that between forty-four thousand and ninety-eight thousand Americans die from medical errors each year. The vast majority of deaths and injuries from such errors were not the fault of negligent doctors or hospitals but the result of outmoded practices, habits, and systems, such as the failure to keep a patient's medications straight. Electronic medical records, patient registries, medication-reminder systems, and reporting and analysis of errors could all raise the quality of care while reducing its costs.

All the cost-saving measures I propose will be good in and of themselves—good for health care, good for employers, good for middle-class families struggling with high premiums and out-of-pocket costs, good for seniors, and good for our economy. And they can also help us take the second big step toward a modern system of health care, expanding coverage to include more Americans.

It's important to understand here that what we spend to extend such coverage will be partially offset by the elimination of the very expensive and often ineffective care the uninsured currently receive. When uninsured people become sick, they often go to emergency rooms, where they are treated at relatively high expense, especially if the care is routine. If they have money, they pay for the care out of pocket; if they don't, the cost, called uncompensated care, is borne by other patients or by the government. It is estimated that Americans as a whole paid out thirty-five billion dollars to cover uncompensated care in 2001, with federal, state, and local governments responsible for 85 percent of the total.

One of the biggest contributing factors to the high number of uninsured Americans is that so many of our small-business owners just can't afford to provide health insurance for their employees—or even themselves. Small businesses by definition simply don't have the purchasing power to get affordable health insurance. And many of them don't have the profit margins to cover their share of the costs even if they could get a decent plan.

✷

Last year I had a personal encounter with the health-care system when I underwent surgery for prostate cancer. My father died of this disease, so I knew I was at risk and received annual PSA screenings. The timing of my diagnosis was problematic, for I had recently announced an exploratory candidacy for president, and in addition to my Senate duties, I was already actively campaigning.

As a U.S. senator I have access to first-class care, and I really didn't worry much about the medical procedure itself. Former senator Bob Dole, who had prostate surgery years earlier, called me up in the hospital and told me I was setting a good example by how calmly I was taking the whole thing. But I know that part of my calm was due simply to the knowledge that I had the best possible care. The surgery was uneventful, and I got through the recovery and back on my feet in just a couple of weeks. I had to take quite a bit of pain medication at first, and after trying to keep up with what I was missing on the Senate floor, I joked to a number of visitors that you haven't lived until you've watched C-SPAN on drugs.

But it certainly dawned on me while I was lying in that hospital bed what the whole experience might have been like if I hadn't been a senator and, worse yet, wasn't covered by health insurance. If I were one of those forty million uninsured Americans, would I have been getting the regular PSA screenings that undoubtedly saved my life? And even if I had discovered the disease before it killed me, would I have made the wisest choice about how to treat it? Or what if my health insurance covered only a fraction of the costs? These questions bothered me then and bother me now. And it's no coincidence that my plan for covering uninsured Americans is based on making sure they have access to the same kind of health insurance members of Congress have.

Nine million federal employees and their families now receive health care through a system that offers a wide choice of affordable coverage options with group protections and good benefits. Under my proposal, everyone from large employers to the self-employed to those who buy coverage as individuals will be able to take part in this system.

Small businesses and their employees will especially benefit from this plan. It would offer both employers and employees tax credits (refundable in the case of employees, which means they get a check if the amount of the credit exceeds their income tax liability) for up to 50 percent of the cost of coverage.

My plan also guarantees that two other categories of especially vulnerable Americans receive and keep health insurance. The first category consists of those who are between jobs, either voluntarily or because they've been laid off—an increasing problem in an economy that's lost so many jobs since President Bush took office. Currently, under the provisions called COBRA, workers who had insurance in their previous jobs have the right to keep it for a period of time—but only if they pay their own and the previous employer's share of the premium, which is a tall order for someone who is out of a job. My plan offers them a tax credit that will cover 75 percent of the cost of continuing their own insurance or buying into the federal employee health plan. The second category that's especially vulnerable consists of people between the ages of fifty-five and sixty-five, who aren't yet eligible for Medicare and find that insurers don't want to cover them if they lose their jobs or retire early. This is the fastest-growing group of the uninsured. Under my plan, they, too, would have both guaranteed access to the federal employee health plan and a tax credit to make that coverage affordable.

Finally, there are millions of self-employed people, independent contractors, contingent workers, and temporary workers who cannot get employer-based coverage and are forced to buy insurance in the very expensive and selective individual-policy market. They, too, would have access to the federal employee health plan under my proposal, along with assistance to cover any health-care costs that exceed 6 percent of their incomes.

Finally, we have to take care of the most vulnerable Americans of all—our kids. And covering virtually all of America's children is the third main goal of my health-care plan.

I do think it's true that we make a decision about nothing less than the future of our country when we decide what if anything we can do to ensure kids a healthy start in life. Today millions of children go without immunizations and regular checkups or without preventive health care or treatment of chronic diseases. That must stop.

But guaranteeing health coverage for kids runs right up

against a roadblock: the fiscal problems of the states. We rely on the states, through Medicaid and the CHIP program, to provide health insurance for children whose parents don't provide it for them—with, of course, the federal government picking up at least half the tab. Today millions of kids are eligible but don't have the coverage, often because their parents don't know about it or don't know how to apply for it. And with the states now in the worst fiscal crisis since World War II, they are pulling back from, rather than extending, efforts to enroll children in their insurance programs. Earlier this year, Congress forced the administration to provide some short-term help for state Medicaid programs as part of the deal that gave the president yet another round of tax cuts aimed at the wealthy, but this step will only help slow the flow of children into the ranks of the uninsured.

I propose a bigger, bolder step: a new deal with the states that stipulates that the federal government will immediately pick up the full cost of insurance for the twenty million children enrolled in the Medicaid program for low-income families. In exchange, the states would have to agree to aggressively sign up children who are eligible for CHIP (which covers kids at a somewhat higher income range, including those of many working families) and expand coverage with the states and federal government both splitting the costs to include their parents as well. Down the road, when states are in better fiscal condition, they would be expected to expand coverage to single and childless adults who are uninsured and live in poverty. This swap would assure that children's health insurance does not depend on whether the economy is thriving. And since every kid would be eligible for health-care coverage, they could be automatically covered, no questions asked. It would also cover millions of their parents and single and childless adults.

Altogether, my health plan would ensure that about 99 percent of America's children and 96 percent of its adults have insurance and would greatly broaden the options for millions of Americans with or without insurance today. It would do so within the context of a systematic effort to hold down health-care costs not by price controls but by market forces, enhanced consumer purchasing power, modern technology, and better medicine and disease management. It would cut both government and private-sector bureaucracy and would leave in place the basic system that most Americans rely on for their health care.

Of course, this is not the only thing we need to do to improve our health-care system. I will be outlining a whole series of ways to make our health-care system fairer. First of all, health insurers should cover mental health services in the same way they cover physical services. For too long our nation has discriminated against people with mental illness. Fortunately, science and research have taught us that mental illnesses are just as treatable as physical illnesses. Now it is time for our health-care system to recognize this as well and that means full parity.

We also need to assure fairness for people with disabilities. Too often people with disabilities who want to go to work cannot because they will lose their health-care coverage and because of their preexisting conditions, won't be able to get it from their employers. In 2000, we started to fix these backward incentives by allowing states to provide health coverage for people with disabilities who returned to work, but we have more to do. We need to pass what is known as the Kennedy-Grassley bill that enables parents of kids with disabilities to go to work and keep their kids on Medicaid. We also need to get rid of some of the institutional biases in the Medicaid program that often mean someone with long-term care needs can get help with nursing home care but not in home services.

We also must treat our seniors with dignity and respect—and that means providing affordable, meaningful prescription drug benefits. We are making so much progress with new medications and therapies that can help our seniors live longer and healthier lives. We must make sure that our seniors can afford these critical medications.

We need to help make health-care services more available to those in underserved areas, including rural areas. We need to expand and strengthen community health centers and provide incentives to health-care providers who serve in these areas. Finally, we need to recruit and train more health-care workers. I authored legislation to help recruit and train more nurses, but it was just a start. We need to treat our health-care workers with dignity—and that means better pay, better treatment, and no mandatory overtime.

These steps are critical to keeping our health-care system the best in the world.

If I seem to be placing more emphasis on the idea of controlling costs and modernizing medicine than some politicians, that's deliberate, for I view modernizing our health-care system and approaching universal coverage as a major intergenerational challenge for our country.

If we can't protect the health of our kids and give them a healthy start in life, we will fail to live up to the great American tradition of lifting each generation higher than the last.

If we don't modernize our health-care system, empower Americans with choices and personal responsibility, and bring costs under control, we will fail to meet the challenge just ahead of the retirement of the baby-boom generation, which will redefine old age as we know it.

And if we don't figure out a way to approach universal health coverage without creating a big government bureaucracy to administer it, we will fail to meet the challenge of making government an instrument for the popular will, which gives Americans the tools they need to solve their own problems but remains the servant, not the master, of the taxpayers who finance its efforts.

I know health care is a complicated issue, and my own plan can't be fully explained in a few phrases. But we have the opportunity, if we act now, to make health care a fairly straightforward matter in the future. Here, in summary form, is my bottom line:

—All Americans will have access to the same health-care coverage that their member of Congress has today.

—A commitment to work until every American has affordable health insurance—starting with a plan that covers 99 percent of children and 96 percent of all Americans.

—Contain soaring health-care costs by making prescription drugs more affordable, getting rid of frivolous lawsuits, reducing uncompensated care, and giving patients affordable health-care choices.

—Relief to employers who offer affordable coverage to their employees by covering a portion of their highest cost cases.

—Save costs by cutting bureaucracy; that cuts nearly $350 billion a year out of the health-care system.

★

Treating patients with dignity is a particular concern for me. Some patients have earned the right to a special measure of respect from everyone involved in their care, including the federal government: our veterans.

Our nation made a solemn covenant with these men and women, who did their part in defending our country. But America has not always done its part for them. About 400,000 qualified veterans are denied access to Veterans Administration health care

*and more than 235,000 veterans already in the system have to
wait six months or more for their first doctor's visit. Many of them
are waiting solely to get a prescription written and filled. That
makes me angry. And it makes me even angrier that the Bush administration is fighting to cut veterans' health benefits at the same
time that it identifies the president with veterans of Operation Iraqi
Freedom and tries to devote nearly a trillion dollars to new tax
cuts for the wealthy Americans whose comfortable lifestyles veterans
have fought to protect. I have already fought this injustice and as
president will fight it even more passionately.*

*There is another category of Americans that deserves the most
from our health-care system but is being shortchanged today: our
seniors.*

*During the last four years, I lost my parents, both of whom
died from chronic diseases. But, thank God, both of them had the
wherewithal and the family support to be able to die with dignity,
surrounded by the people who had been the beneficiaries of their
love and had shared their lives for many decades.*

*I think all our parents deserve this support and this dignity. And
that's another reason we need a health-care system that's not just about
profits, rules of eligibility, rationing care, or the needs of the various
professionals who earn their living in health care. We need a system
that's full of people like the Brockton nurses, who put patients first.*

✶

I'm passionate about my health-care plan because health
care has been a major blind spot in our society for years and
one of the very few things that gives one pause in confi-

dently declaring our country the greatest place on earth. That's why we need a modernized health-care system that builds on what is uniquely American: our unsurpassed ingenuity and technology, our high standards of care, our preference for choice and competition, our belief in equal treatment, and our passion for excellence and efficiency. I want to build on what works and fix what doesn't in our health-care system. I want to combine traditional American values with twenty-first-century science and technology, giving every American the opportunity and responsibility to take advantage of the unprecedented advances in life-giving medicine that American scientists and health-care providers have pioneered. And I want to call Americans to rise to the challenge of accessible and affordable health care for all.

The Challenge of Defending the Environment and Achieving Energy Independence

These two topics should be considered together for three important reasons: The first and most obvious is that the best way to protect our environment is to change the way we generate energy to light, heat, and cool our homes, power our factories, and offices and to transport us from home to work and back. The second reason is that protecting the environment and securing energy independence represent a common challenge to America's values and interests—a challenge to our love for our country, both for the physical space we inhabit and the freedom we prize at home and abroad. The third reason I address them together is that they are national priorities that have been equally abandoned by the Bush administration, despite its mollifying words on the environment and its tough rhetoric on national security.

It's taken a real effort by the administration and right-wing ideologues to get these issues so profoundly wrong.

On the environment, their rationalization is that doing the right thing would hurt our economy. And they've assured us that our dependence on foreign oil sources can be overcome only by deepening our dependence on domestic sources.

Both their claims are factually incorrect and morally flawed.

The last three decades have demonstrated with compelling evidence that cleaning up our environment will strengthen, not weaken, our economy. We don't, in fact, have to make a choice between jobs and the environment. In fact, protecting the environment will only help generate jobs—the high-value-added jobs of the future.

Meanwhile, the idea of drilling our way to energy independence with our own resources is just ludicrous. There's not enough domestic oil available in the near future to do anything but make us even more dependent on global markets where supplies and prices are ultimately controlled by Middle East producers.

The president and his appointees are taking this country in the wrong direction on the environment and energy. They are listening to extremist voices—the kind of people who deny, against all the evidence, that there's any such thing as global warming and who are willing to gamble the future of the planet and the lives of all those who live on it to prove they are right. The administration is also following the advice of narrow interests—especially those associated with the oil industry (from which both the president and vice president have profited), which view environmental protection and energy independence alike as threats to their bottom line.

A Kerry administration will put America back into the mainstream of respect for scientific evidence, technological progress, and bipartisan action on energy and the environment. Those who deny our responsibility for stewardship of the earth and its resources will be dismissed from positions of influence. And while there are legitimate differences of opinion on many issues of environmental and energy policy, I will not tolerate, much less invite into the White House to craft policies, special pleaders seeking government-imposed privileges to despoil the earth or control our energy supplies.

All too often, Congress has viewed environmental and energy policies as regional problems, battles to be fought between those who allegedly gain or lose from this or that strategy. I, in turn, am committed to building a national consensus based on the national interest to pursue a smart and effective strategy for a cleaner environment and energy independence.

Concern for the environment is a value that was inculcated in me early on. My mother organized recycling in our community back when it was considered little more than an antilitter initiative. She helped build a nature trail. She made me stop my frenetic activity as a child and take the time to appreciate walks in the woods and

other simple experiences of nature. When I was in college, like millions of other Americans I read Rachel Carson's Silent Spring *and for the first time understood that we could lose the beauty and bounty of nature if we didn't take common responsibility for doing something about lakes full of toxins and rivers that caught fire.*

In 1970, shortly after I returned from Vietnam, I took part in the first Earth Day in Massachusetts. On that day no one thought of environmentalism as a specifically Democratic or liberal movement. It was, rather, a shared commitment of all civic-minded Americans, who might nonetheless have legitimate differences of opinion about how to go about safeguarding our air, water, and land. Our collective mood was one of concern, not anger, and it never occurred to any of us in 1970 that there was some fundamental contradiction between a free-market economy or a high standard of living and taking practical measures to conserve the resources that made growth possible in the first place.

It is worth recalling that it was Richard Nixon who signed the Clean Air and Clean Water Acts into law. Two of my early heroes as environmentalists were Republicans: Interior Secretary Walter Hickel and the first Environmental Protection Agency director, William Ruckelshaus. Most New Englanders in both parties regarded the environmental movement as a natural extension of good citizenship—and for that matter, of basic respect for God's creation.

It wasn't really until the 1980s that environmental issues became genuinely controversial, then gradually partisan, and finally as toxic as the worst poisons being unleashed upon the earth. I think we would all benefit from another stretch of time when the political atmosphere is more as it was in 1970—when, to paraphrase Kermit the Frog, it seemed much easier to be green.

★

I remain a convinced optimist when it comes to the question of whether we can make serious environmental progress while maintaining robust economic growth and the freedom to live responsible lives as we choose. That optimism is in large part a reflection of what we've already accomplished in the thirty-three years since that first Earth Day.

We removed lead from gasoline and all but eliminated lead from our air. We took aim at other sources of air pollution and cut smog by about a third despite a rise in the number of cars and industrial plants. We more than doubled the percentage of lakes and rivers that are judged safe to fish or swim in. We cut acid rain nearly in half. We've shut down hundreds of toxic waste sites and cleaned up nearly half of those that remain. We saved the bald eagle, the gray whale, and the peregrine falcon from extinction. Famously dirty places like Boston Harbor in my own home town have largely been cleaned up. And the Cuyahoga River in Cleveland no longer catches fire.

I think we've proved beyond any reasonable doubt over the last few decades that a good environment, a sound economy, and a high quality of life not only can but must go hand in hand. But despite such remarkable achievements, old problems like smog and rainwater pollution and deforestation are obviously on the rise again, and new and potentially catastrophic problems like global climate change call for bold and novel actions. Instead of rising to meet this challenge of defending our national heritage of air, water, and land from polluters, however, the president and his appointees have all too often unconditionally surrendered to the demands of polluters.

Reversing nearly two decades of progress on toxic waste sites, the administration has abandoned the polluter-pays principle for financing the Superfund cleanup system, which means the fund will soon run dry and cleanups will stop. About seven thousand people live within a mile of a site in my home state of Massachusetts that contains cyanide, heavy metals, pesticides, and PCBs. The Bush administration is doing nothing to help them. That must change.

Reversing his campaign pledge to support limits on carbon dioxide emissions from power plants, the president allowed utilities to decide voluntarily whether they wanted to clean up their operations—a backward-looking policy to which the administration gave the Orwellian name of the Clear Skies Initiative. Not only will this action contribute to the potential catastrophe of global climate change; it will also reverse our progress on acid rain and smog, causing asthma, heart disease, and neurological damage to untold thousands of Americans whose only mistake is to breathe.

The retrograde environmental agenda of the administration marches under other false flags, like the Healthy Forest initiative aimed at massively increasing logging activity and safe drinking water "reforms" that infamously included an increase in allowable levels of arsenic.

As a counter to this trend, I can begin by promising

that I will work to enforce our environmental laws, not help industry lobbyists find ways around them. And at the same time, I will do everything within my power to encourage the private sector to come up with ways to make environmental improvements not only less costly and more efficient but even profitable. America has long been and ought to remain the leading source of green technologies that make producing everything from energy to cars cleaner and cheaper at the same time. And those green technologies themselves can and should become major high-wage industries in their own right.

We need tougher, smarter enforcement in part simply to keep up with new dangers to our environment and our health. There are some eighty thousand chemicals registered for use in the United States, and each day Americans are exposed to hundreds, even thousands of them. They are released into our air, water, and land and into our food chain. We bring them into our homes in the produce and products we buy, the cleaners we use in our kitchens, the cosmetics we apply to our bodies, and the toys our children play with. But less than 10 percent of these chemicals have been tested. Some have been linked to cancer, birth defects, and infertility.

If I'm elected president, I will give the EPA and the Food and Drug Administration the authority and the money to keep pace with these new sustances and test them before they enter our homes, our lives, and our bodies. It makes me laugh when some of our right-wing friends dismiss this sort of minimum public safety measure as big government. Anything less should be considered *bad* government, because it represents government under the thumb of special interests.

Another basic step we have to take is to help cities and counties keep pace with the fundamental infrastructure necessary to treat sewage and keep polluted runoff out of our rivers, lakes, and harbors. With state and local governments facing a terrible fiscal crisis, it will be tempting, if not necessary, for many of them to postpone repairs and replacements of water or sewer lines or wastewater treatment facilities. The Bush administration has been very reluctant to pitch in and help. This, too, must change.

These are minimal steps that can be taken to avoid a reversal of what we have accomplished in the past in protecting the environment from intentional damage by polluters and unintentional damage through negligence and a failure of national vision. But we need to raise our sights much higher to deal with new environmental threats, which we must convert into new environmental opportunities. The most controversial of these, of course, is the challenge of global climate change and the greenhouse gas emissions that scientists are increasingly certain contribute to it.

Even if I were not an environmentalist, I would distinctly remember the Rio Summit of 1991, which laid the initial groundwork for what later became the Kyoto Protocol on global climate change.

That conference remains so vivid in my memory because it's where I first spent a lot of time with my future wife, Teresa.

It was a good moment for our country as well as for my personal life. In a continuation of the great bipartisan tradition of environmentalism, George H. W. Bush made a commitment at Rio to the United States' assuming a role of leadership in meeting the challenge of global climate change and addressing the broader issue of an international consensus on sustainable development. He understood clearly that if America did not lead by precept and by example on these issues, there was no hope at all for voluntary action by developing countries to avoid catastrophic damage to their environments as they began to industrialize.

I came home from Rio proud of our nation's leadership and more aware than ever of the complexity of both global climate change and the challenge of sustainable development. It scarcely occurred to me that President Bush's own party—much less his own son—would soon cave in to the far right's denial that these problems even exist.

The abrupt abandonment of U.S. leadership on these environmental issues has been one of the most disastrous steps taken by George W. Bush's administration, affecting not only our environment but our alliances and our international reputation.

When President Clinton signed the Kyoto Protocol in 1998, he made it clear that the rough goals and guidelines it outlined for action by the United States to reduce its greenhouse gas emissions associated with global warming needed to be revised. When President Bush took office in 2001, he had a clear mandate from the U.S. Senate to continue negotiations on this subject. But instead the president unilaterally repudiated the Kyoto Protocol, calling it "dead on arrival," and indicated no interest in an alternative process for reopening negotiations.

His remarks were instantly reported by media around the world, their underlying contempt all too clear even when translated into dozens of languages. Their impact came back to haunt us when we tried to build a "coalition of the willing" to help us deal with Saddam Hussein. The administration failed to see that Kyoto was not merely a standard diplomatic agreement but an ongoing process that represented the resolve of 160 nations that had worked together for ten years, a group that was convened and led by the United States. It was a good-faith effort that the president simply dismissed, with no effort to mend it, seek compromise, or even discuss it.

Shocked as I was at the time, I wasn't yet aware that the new administration had bought into the right-wing theory that global warming was a hoax perpetrated by radical tree huggers who wanted to use the issue as a way to regulate U.S. businesses and slow growth. As part of its strategy to accommodate the Republican Party's conservative base, the administration ignored the increasingly solid scientific consensus that greenhouse gas emissions (especially the carbon dioxide released by power plants and automobiles) were contributing significantly to climate changes that could eventually wreak havoc on our weather, our coastlines, our water and food supplies, and on our general quality of life.

At one point after his unilateral abandonment of the Kyoto process, the president announced that he would commission a study by the National Academy of Science to assess the evidence for global climate change and its link to greenhouse gas emissions. When the NAS promptly came back with a study that confirmed what most of us already knew along with an expression of urgency about the need for immediate action, the president publicly rejected their conclusions as the work of "the bureaucracy." We had come a very long way down since Rio, and by the time the deeply humiliated EPA director, the former New Jersey governor Christine Todd Whitman, handed in her resignation in the spring of 2003, it was clear that this president had fully abandoned the proud environmentalist tradition of the Republican Party. Instead, he cast his lot with the know-nothings and the do-nothings whose agendas coincided with the interests of America's and the world's worst polluters.

What makes the Kyoto situation especially frustrating is that we already have experience in the effectiveness of multilateral cooperation in addressing environmental problems. It's no secret that my experiences in Vietnam have led me, along with other Vietnam vets in the Senate, like John McCain, to feel a special responsibility for healing relations between our two countries.

Because it united two of my ongoing passions in public policy, I reached out to the World Bank a few years ago to help organize the first conference on sustainable development to be held in Southeast Asia. The idea was to assist Vietnam's leadership and people in taking a fresh look at how the country was developing, at a time when Hanoi was in danger of becoming another Beijing, a city whose air is so dirty that its residents commonly wore surgical masks on the streets long before the advent of SARS.

We brought corporate executives, scientists, and engineers from around the world to the table with the Vietnamese to discuss how that country could find cleaner ways to develop and keep higher incomes in tandem with higher standards for air, land, and water quality.

I don't understand why the United States isn't taking this sort of initiative all over the world. I don't understand why efforts to raise environmental standards don't accompany our attempts to open up new markets for trade and investment and spur greater development in places like Africa and Asia. And I don't understand why President Bush doesn't comprehend that the countries that want to work with us on protecting the environment are the same countries that can work with us to rid the world of terrorism.

We must also be mindful that while we all share the responsibility to act as stewards of our environment, some of us bear an unfair share of the cost of ignoring that responsibility.

I am especially worried, for example, about the health

consequences of inadequate research on and safeguards against toxic substances in our environment. As part of her work as chairman of the Heinz Family Philanthropies, my wife, Teresa, has sponsored groundbreaking research on the consequences of pollution and other environmental hazards for women's health. There's nothing abstract or speculative about the links she's found between toxic substances and significantly increased risks for breast cancer and other potentially fatal conditions for women.

Similarly, it's time to take concrete action based on our knowledge that the neighborhoods where low-income and minority Americans live are disproportionately affected by environmental abuses. African Americans, for example, have shorter life expectancies and face greater risks for respiratory illness, heart disease, and other debilitating conditions because of where they live. We certainly cannot celebrate our progress in eliminating overt racism and other forms of discrimination if we have simply replaced poisonous laws and poisonous attitudes with a poisonous environment.

The problem of what many have called environmental injustice is well documented. Back in 1983, the General Accounting Office determined that most landfills in eight southern states were located near mostly minority communities. A few years later, a study by the United Church of Christ's Commission on Racial Justice found that this wasn't just a southern phenomenon; the location of waste facilities was highly correlated with the presence of low-income and minority populations all over the country. And in 1992, a federal investigation launched by the first Bush administration confirmed that the poor face greater risk of hazardous waste exposure and sustain more environmental costs than more fortunate Americans.

In 1994 President Clinton signed an executive order acknowledging environmental justice as a national concern and requiring all federal agencies to address the needs of those disproportionately affected by it, including farm workers exposed to insecticides, poor children exposed to lead paint in old buildings, and minority citizens living near hazardous-waste incinerators. But little has been done to act on this order.

On Earth Day 2003, I announced a proposal to resume the battle against environmental injustice, in part by greatly elevating it as a priority for the EPA and other federal enforcement agencies and in part by creating environmental empowerment zones, in which the impact of federal decisions on the health of low-income and minority citizens would have to be taken into account before they are implemented.

I also called for a measure that will be critical not only in dealing with environmental injustice but also in dealing with environmental health issues generally: establishing a national tracking system for chronic diseases and environmental health hazards. Where evidence exists to link diseases to environmental causes, we need to know much more about their incidence if we are to craft an effective response to them.

The impact of toxic materials and pollution on the

places where Americans live is only one element of a larger consideration: the impact of where Americans live on the quality of life in this country. Developing countries aren't the only ones that need to practice sustainable development. Environmental improvements must go hand in hand with land-use policies that preserve green spaces and farmlands and reduce the suburban sprawl that is making many of our major metropolitan areas less and less habitable.

In the Senate I've worked for years to expand the resources we devote to the Land and Water Conservation Fund, which helps states and communities protect parks and open spaces without dictation from Washington. And I've also been a big supporter of conservation efforts to protect wetlands, wildlife habitats, grasslands, and farmlands.

But protecting our open spaces is just part of what we need to do to build truly livable communities. In the early stages of his 2000 presidential campaign Al Gore was ridiculed for talking about sprawl and traffic congestion, which were viewed by critics as a yuppie issue that could emerge only at a time of unparalleled prosperity. And in fact, Al didn't discuss it in the general election campaign nearly as much as he might have. I'm here to tell you this is a real issue, an issue of concern in good times and bad. After all, Americans don't just work for a cash income—they work for a standard of living. And when their quality of life declines because their neighborhood is surrounded by strip malls or because the time it takes to get to work and back home has suddenly tripled, it becomes a subject they care about, and public authorities should respond accordingly.

I do not believe that Washington should be in the business of telling local communities how to organize themselves, but we can at least respect the principle of doing no harm by examining federal policies, especially in the transportation area, to make sure that we are not subsidizing sprawl. We should not, for example, push states and localities to build new roads at the edge of metropolitan areas when the same dollars could be used to repair and expand existing roads closer to urban centers. And while the federal government should likewise not get involved in local land-use planning, we should, as Al Gore proposed, help cities and counties, especially in rural areas, with resources to draw up their own plans.

But everything you and I can think of to get America back on track toward a sound environmental policy won't amount to much if we don't deal with the single greatest cause of our environmental problems and a direct and growing threat to our national security: our excessive dependence on the wrong energy sources, controlled by the wrong people.

We've known for a very long time that our heavy reliance on petroleum products and other fossil fuels has been terrible for the environment. With the growing evidence of global climate change, the potential price of our oil addiction has grown from the exorbitant to the horrifying. And we've known at least since the early 1970s that depending on oil as a primary energy source has exposed us to the risk of supply interruptions, price shocks, economic chaos, and political blackmail from a well-organized cartel centered in the Middle East.

The Bush administration's primary energy strategy has actually increased our dependence on the consumption of oil while pointing vaguely to some distant day when hydrogen fuel cell technology may make it possible to entirely replace oil in the transportation sector. Perhaps only an oilman like George Bush advised by another oilman—Dick Cheney—could have formulated such a policy. (Perhaps it's simply another version of the administration's fiscal strategy: running up big federal budget deficits as a way to create an impotent federal government.)

The truth is that, with 65 percent of the world's oil reserves located in the Middle East, our overreliance on oil is a real threat to our national security. Even if we manage to pump more of it here and import less of it from there, Middle Eastern oil producers will still control the world markets that set prices everywhere, including the United States. And while the administration's pump-it-up strategy doesn't guarantee much in the way of new domestic oil production at any time in the immediate future, it will cause immediate damage to the Arctic National Wildlife Reserve and other environmentally sensitive and nationally significant public lands.

It's time to issue an American declaration of independence from oil. We spend twenty billion dollars a year on oil imports from the Persian Gulf. Too often these funds pour into the pockets of some of the planet's most uncooperative and repressive regimes. And they can too easily be diverted to finance the very terrorists who seek to destroy us. Even at home, we spend billions in taxpayers' dollars for unnecessary subsidies for domestic oil production. We need a new strategy that's consistent with our energy needs, our environmental needs, our economic needs, and our national security needs.

Instead of more oil today and hydrogen fuel cells in an indefinite tomorrow, I've called for the peaceful equivalent of a new Manhattan Project to begin the process of creating a foundation for energy independence and an oil-free future.

Sixty-one years ago, Franklin Roosevelt brought together America's best minds and most innovative technologies in a crash project to develop a nuclear weapon before one could be developed and deployed by the fascist powers. It was called the Manhattan Project because it was launched in New York (about a block, in fact, from where the World Trade Center towers once stood).

I've borrowed this term for my energy independence proposal because it conveys the right sense of urgency and focus and the right combination of public resources and private innovation that we need today.

My strategy calls for new investments in research; new incentives for companies and consumers; new partnerships across all the old dividing lines of government, business, and academia; and higher standards of energy efficiency to be met by both business and government.

The goal is simple but revolutionary: for the first time

in human history, to harness the natural world around us to light and power the world we live in. The sun, the wind, water, and a rich array of crops can provide us with secure forms of energy at reasonable costs for a modern twenty-first-century economy.

Until we reach that degree of sustainability and even after we do so, we can use new technologies and innovations to recast existing sources of energy—like oil, coal, and natural gas—so that we consume them more cleanly and efficiently. And by seizing the amazing opportunities presented to us by American agriculture, we can make the renewable fuel content of gasoline grow to five billion gallons in the next decade.

As a senator from a New England state, I'm especially sensitive to concerns about energy supplies and prices. We're the ultimate energy-consuming region, with virtually no production, little diversity in sources, and a lot of dark days and tough winter weather to force up prices. It wasn't always that way, for Massachusetts was pretty much the Texas or Oklahoma of the early nineteenth century, when it provided much of America with light through whale oil.

I remember that back during the big energy crisis of the 1970s, when fuel oil supplies were low and prices were skyrocketing, there was a bumper sticker that was popular in the Southwest that said, "Drive fast and freeze a Yankee." We Boston Red Sox fans interpreted that to our advantage.

As lieutenant governor of Massachusetts in the early 1980s,

I worked with my counterparts in other states with similar deficiencies and needs to ensure that national energy policy did not pass us by or pass along disproportionate costs. At the time I kept thinking: Why isn't there a truly national strategy for energy instead of a messy compromise among our regional strategies?

Part of what excites me about a new strategy for renewable energy sources is that it may finally begin to break down the regional differences of interest and opinion and create a genuine national consensus on energy. Water, wind, and sun are available resources—in varying degrees, of course—all over the country. There's arable land in every region. There are a lot more natural-gas reserves in more parts of the country there than is oil.

With so many resources so close at hand, we can all be Texas. Hell, we can all be Saudi Arabia. And we can all get along.

★

Because I believe it's important to be comprehensive in energy policy, there are five planks in my strategy for energy independence.

First, I propose taking some of the royalties that corporations now pay for the right to drill for oil on public lands and dedicate them to research into and development of cleaner and more abundant energy sources. This new energy security and conservation fund will invest in promoting rapid growth in technologies that save energy and create alternative fuels, from hydrogen fuel cells to biomass projects that use agricultural byproducts to generate energy.

The underlying rationale here is to create for the first time a guaranteed national commitment to reduce our dependence on foreign oil, with a dedicated trust fund to help pay for its costs.

Second, I propose a new push to make our cars and trucks more energy-efficient by reducing petroleum use in the long interim period before hydrogen fuel cell technology truly becomes a viable alternative.

Today a car fueled by hydrogen costs up to a half million dollars, and we've only begun to figure out a system for safely storing and distributing hydrogen fuel. To speed up the process of making this technology more practical, I will create a new hydrogen institute that will enlist America's scientists and researchers in both the public and private sectors, fund research, and design the codes and standards that will ensure the safety of a new hydrogen economy. My goal is to put 100,000 hydrogen-powered vehicles on the road by 2010 and 2.5 million by 2020.

But in the meantime, we do not dare delay, as the Bush administration wishes to, other energy-conservation measures until hydrogen fuel technology becomes feasible. We cannot leave our security, our jobs, and our environment vulnerable until then.

Because one out of every seven barrels of oil in the world is consumed on America's highways, they are the battleground where the fight for energy independence must begin. We already have the technology to manufacture cars that give far better gas mileage. What we lack is the will, the leadership, and the right incentives to make them a reality. The initial set of fuel efficiency standards that were issued decades ago helped break the back of the first energy crisis, and our auto producers and auto workers rose to the occasion with a new generation of cars that performed better using less energy. We can achieve the same efficiency again while giving Americans the kinds of vehicles they wish to drive. My plan includes both economic incentives to build the cars, SUVs, and buses of the future and higher standards for gas mileage for every new vehicle produced or sold in this country. It also will invest one billion dollars a year to help our auto industry convert to new plants to build more energy-efficient vehicles and includes tax incentives for consumers to buy them.

Higher but realistic standards and incentives to reach them will serve to strengthen the American auto industry, protect and create jobs, safeguard our environment, and ultimately wean our nation from reliance on Middle Eastern oil.

The third plank in my energy independence plan is to launch our country's first really systematic effort to tap renewable energy sources, reserves that are almost infinite.

The clear goal I want to set is that we be able to produce 20 percent of our electricity from the wind, the sun, and forest and farm products by 2020.

We can reach this goal in part by channeling federal dollars into research to realize the unlimited promise of novel forms of deriving ethanol from biomass, creating an entirely new cash crop for America's farms and commercial forestries while we're at it. We must also spur more private-sector investment in clean-energy projects and should make tax credits available to prime this particular pump.

Most important, the federal government itself can lead the way and use its enormous purchasing power to bring about change—a general principle of a Kerry administration and one that's of particular importance in this area. With five hundred thousand buildings under his jurisdiction and a huge fleet of cars, Uncle Sam is the largest single consumer of energy in the entire world. With the right leadership, we can demonstrate better than any other single party all the environmental and financial savings attainable by energy efficiency. As president, I will demand that the federal government take steps to cut its energy bill 20 percent by 2020—and will challenge state and local governments, corporations, universities, small businesses, and hospitals to do the same.

And I will encourage Americans to incorporate these efficiencies into their own lives. I will propose tax credits for builders and homeowners to make homes meet the highest energy-efficiency standards, which will cut utility bills every month for millions of families. And I will offer more Americans a real choice of public transportation options to get them to work and back more rapidly, at a lower cost, and with less pollution.

The fourth plank in my strategy for energy independence is to pursue a comprehensive effort to expand supplies of natural gas, the cleanest and most American (90 percent of our consumption is from domestic sources) of fossil fuels.

Today high prices and supply shortages are hurting

families that depend on natural gas to heat, cool, and light their homes and are also hurting businesses and farms that rely on it for a variety of purposes. Because part of the problem is caused by profiteers that manipulate natural gas markets across boundaries, I want to create a North American compact on natural gas. We would form a partnership with Canada and Mexico to develop and transport clean natural gas from all over the continent, especially from Alaska and the Gulf of Mexico.

The fifth plank of my strategy for energy independence is to restore the place of coal as a valuable resource and help it shed its longtime image of having a negative impact on the environment. As with raising the fuel efficiency for our automobiles and trucks, the technologies already exist—or can soon be developed—to generate clean electrical power from coal. These would enable us to clean up pollution from power plants without abandoning the coal industry or the families and communities that depend on it. I'm tired of the scare tactics used by some Republicans to convince people in areas especially dependent on one source of energy either for jobs or their own use that protecting the environment or achieving energy independence is too expensive for them and for the country. That's not only untrue but it's not the American way of addressing problems.

In pursuing every part of my energy plan, I also want to rethink federal programs and investments, many of which are layered like the fossil remains of earlier phases of national energy policy. I don't want to spend *more* on energy; I want to spend *smarter*. And no existing item in the tax code or the federal budget will be sacred anymore. For decades we've been lavishing billions of dollars in subsidies and corporate welfare on big energy companies while starving the researchers and consumers who could power our way to energy independence. Unfortunately, the oilmen at the top of the Bush administration seem to want only to do more—much more—of the same.

My favorite example of an energy tax incentive gone badly wrong is a one-hundred-thousand-dollar tax break available for the purchase of luxury gas guzzlers like the Hummer. It was originally intended to help farmers and others who need light trucks in their work or to get to remote homes. Now it represents a taxpayer subsidy for continued energy dependence.

My bottom line is that we need to renew our faith in the American people to accomplish big things in the national interest in a short period of time. Like the Manhattan Project, we need an effort that brings together our best minds from every walk of life and concentrates their talents on a clear set of tangible goals. Like John F. Kennedy's challenge to place a man on the moon, our challenge is to make energy independence a major, audacious, shared national enterprise.

My plan would break the back of our dependence on oil and foreign manipulation of our energy supplies, our economy, and our national security posture in the Middle East and elsewhere. It would put us on the fast track to a future where most of our energy needs are met from clean, domestic, and renewable sources. It would radically reduce pollution, especially the greenhouse gases that scientists believe contribute so much to potentially catastrophic global climate change. And it would be good, not bad, for our economy, creating, by my estimate, five hundred thousand new jobs around the country.

Most of all, my proposals on both energy and environmental protection will place these subjects back on the front burner of the national debate where they belong and where they will be of integral importance to our budget policy, trade policy, and foreign policy.

Sometimes I'm asked—sometimes I even ask myself—if engaging the country and the opposition on so wide a range of policy issues is a good idea. Many political strategists think that talking about more than one or two issues is confusing or ineffective in a world where most voters have little time or attention to spend on government or politics. They also say it's a mistake to get into any level of specificity on issues like the environment and energy, which necessarily involve scientific or technological terminology, unless you are in front of an audience with a special interest in them.

I think the presidency of George W. Bush has produced a resounding retort to that kind of question and that kind of thinking. Too many important issues have simply been left off this administration's agenda and hence are absent from this president's dialogue with the American people. Too many of the challenges we face are too interconnected with one another to be ignored—such as the national security risks we take if we turn our back on global environmental issues or tolerate dependence on unstable countries for our energy supplies. Simplistic or single-issue approaches to our national challenges aren't simply inadequate; they are often dead wrong.

I also reject the idea of discussing particular issues only with narrow audiences that have a special interest in those issues, whether it's the noble interest of idealistic advocates or the ignoble interest of those looking to make a buck on public policies. You can't build a strong progressive agenda supported by a majority of Americans by putting together a long string of special appeals to narrow groups with no common values, vision, or goals. Even if I could, I wouldn't want to.

I love talking with environmentalists, beginning with my wife. What I love even more is talking someone who's not an environmentalist into caring about our environment and understanding it as a common resource and the responsibility of all citizens. Each time that happens, we secure not merely one more vote for a proenvironment candidate but one more active citizen who will no longer accept a government that consigns big chunks of public life and national resources to special interests because they're the only ones who are paying attention.

As I learned many years ago as a young prosecutor in Middlesex County, Massachusetts, building active citizenship is in some ways like fighting crime. If you get law-abiding citizens to insist on their right to use public spaces like parks, streets, subways, sports facilities, and downtown shopping areas, you've won half the fight, because you now outnumber the predators so they tend to stay away. The same is true of public policy. If you get citizens engaged in the full array of issues, the public interest will soon outweigh the special interests, and you will truly have a commonwealth in action.

The Challenge of Reviving
Democracy and Citizenship

★

My generation of Americans—the baby-boom generation—has been blessed to witness some of the greatest tri-
umphs for freedom in human history. Some of us were
born just before or just after America led the fight to crush
fascism and then built the multilateral institutions and alliances designed to supplant fascism and oppose communism with a creed of political and economic freedom. Most
of us saw the decline and fall of European colonialism in
Asia and Africa and the end of Jim Crow in America.

All of us lived through the stunning collapse of communism, beginning with the tearing down of the Berlin
Wall and the breakup of the Soviet Union.

All of us have also observed the rise of religious fun-
damentalism in the Middle East as a new threat to the modern civilization we represent. We've accepted the proposition
that American values, liberties, institutions, products, and
services have become dominant cultural factors in the

world. And we've all accepted that 9/11 represents a full-frontal attack on American ideals of freedom, equality, democracy, and tolerance.

Our primary generational experience has been the validation of what used to be called Western liberal democracy as the best way yet discovered for the government of human beings. While this as been a tremendous reinforcement of our values, at the same time it has presented a tremendous challenge to our willingness to live up to them at home and abroad. And that's why I'm making this challenge part of my candidacy for president.

If we are to stand as the world's role model for freedom, we need to remain vigilant about our own civil liberties. If we are to stand as the world's role model for democracy, we need to become vigilant about participation in our own democratic system. If we are to stand as the world's role model for citizenship, we need to become far more focused on what we expect American citizens to give back in exchange for the blessings of freedom and justice.

Service to this nation has been the defining principle of my own life, and I believe that service can define the life of the nation itself. That means reviving all the civic virtues and institutions we urge the rest of the world to emulate. Visiting this country more than a hundred and fifty years ago, Alexis de Tocqueville observed that America is great because Americans are good. That hasn't changed. But despite all the influence we've had on the world, we still have trouble living up to our own values, our own institutions, our own traditions, and indeed our own goodness. Especially at a time when we are again actively shining our light against the darkness and offering our example to the world, it's time to renew our democracy and our spirit of citizenship here at home.

Some may find it strange that I cite greater vigilance toward civil liberties as a key step in that process. But as we are learning all over again in post–Saddam Iraq, a major element of self-government for any society lies in its recognition of rights for minorities and limitations on state power, reflecting a pervasive habit of mutual respect among all citizens. These qualities can and must be reflected in written laws and constitutions, and they must also be supported by all the institutions of civil society. And to use a biblical phrase, they must be written in our hearts as well.

That's important to remember today, because the war on terrorism is making us reflect anew on the proper balance between government's responsibility to protect all Americans from violence and its responsibility to protect all Americans against violations of their constitutional rights.

I voted for the USA Patriot Act in the Senate right after 9/11 to advance our security at home but I am concerned that Attorney General John Ashcroft's Justice Department is abusing the powers conferred on it by that act, especially in targeting immigrants for scrutiny and detention. More generally, I think the Bush administration is relying far too much on extraordinary police powers and not enough on regular policing in its homeland security efforts, a result of its ideologically driven obsession with eliminating federal assistance to local law enforcement.

And I'm genuinely alarmed at what I've seen of the Patriot II Act, which the administration has not formally unveiled as of this writing. One of its provisions would apparently enable federal authorities to strip U.S. citizens of their rights without due process. More broadly, it would create a separate, very shadowy justice system for terrorist suspects in which most of the rights and procedures normally guaranteed criminal suspects can be abrogated at the discretion of the government.

As a former prosecutor and something of a specialist in dealing with international drug and terror networks, I know there's a big difference between giving the government the resources and commonsense leeway it needs to track a tough and devious foe and giving in to the temptation of taking shortcuts that will sacrifice liberties cheaply without significantly enhancing the effectiveness of law enforcement. Patriot II threatens to cross that line—and to a serious degree. As president, I wouldn't propose it, and if it were passed I would veto it.

Rededicating ourselves to protecting civil liberties means more, however, than merely making sure we don't reduce them in the war on terrorism. It also means making sure that we respect them for all Americans in a clear and consistent way.

For example, it's long past the time that we confer full citizenship rights upon gay and lesbian Americans. And it's important that we perceive the issue in exactly that way—as a simple matter of ensuring that American citizens are treated equally.

Some people—including, unfortunately, the president of the United States—argue that recognizing the rights of gays and lesbians in effect confers special privileges on them. That's just another way of saying that the law will be blind to discrimination if it is based on sexual orientation, and that's simply wrong.

No law can make people approve of gays and lesbians if they believe their moral code forbids them to do so, although as a Christian, I believe that this and every other form of discrimination is opposed to the spirit of the Bible. But if the law cannot command approval, it can demand respect, and that's what I'm calling for in supporting equal treatment of gays and lesbians in employment law and employee benefits, in the right to form domestic partnerships and civil unions, and in the right to raise children.

My attitude toward offering special measures to outlaw discrimination is probably rooted in my experiences with Americans with disabilities. These date back to my first adult advocacy work and to a subject that is still one of my passions: recognizing the debt we owe to our veterans, especially our disabled ones.

Determining precisely what special measures are necessary to ensure equal opportunity is sometimes a difficult process, but it is

*often just a matter of common sense. Some years ago at a public
meeting in Massachusetts, I encountered a small group of disabled
retirees who spent part of the winter in their RVs down in Florida.
They explained to me that the handicapped-parking access licenses
issued by the Commonwealth of Massachusetts weren't recognized
in Florida or in many of the states between Boston and Tampa, forcing them either to go through multiple application processes, be hit
with tickets, or painfully make their way to restaurants or bath-
rooms from the closest available space (which might be quite a dis-
tance away). I asked my staff to investigate the issue. We discovered
that there was no national system for reciprocity in handicap park-
ing permits. I introduced legislation in the Senate to set up such a
system and led it into law. Now nobody thinks twice about it.*

*Should that sort of special measure for a defined category of
Americans be thought of as a privilege that other Americans might
resent? I think not. Ending discrimination should never be considered a special measure; it should be our common duty as a society.*

I feel strongly about extending equal rights to every American. I feel even more strongly about guarding against back-
tracking on civil rights. The ongoing effort to roll back
affirmative action in colleges and universities and in the
workplace has so far been rebuffed by the Supreme Court.
But we're only one appointee away from seeing this campaign succeed. Of course, some employers and some universities have used a poorly tailored or hamhanded system

of preferences that appear to transfer opportunities from one group of people to another instead of expanding opportunities for all. But President Clinton got it right: We should mend, not end, affirmative action.

And I am equally concerned about a particular threat that we now face to a woman's right to choose. Although they don't often discuss it in mixed company, President Bush and the Republican Party are committed to an especially harsh policy of reversing *Roe* v. *Wade*. Some are actually seeking to prohibit abortion and, for that matter, the use of certain birth-control measures by what they call a Human Life Amendment to the United States Constitution.

Since that's not going to happen, the right-to-life movement's fallback position is to change the makeup of the Supreme Court and overturn the constitutional protection for the right to choose. You do not have to believe in the existence of right-wing conspiracies to recognize that there is a clear if quiet understanding between George W. Bush and right-to-life activists that he will do everything possible if Supreme Court openings occur to add the estimated two justices it will take to achieve their desired result. It was his tacit support that led them to side with George W. Bush so completely and so passionately—indeed, resorting to all sorts of underhanded tactics and dirty tricks—during his battle with John McCain for the Republican presidential nomination in 2000. Given the age of several of the justices, it's very likely that there will be at least two openings on the court during the next presidential term. It seems highly unlikely to me that a president who's been so focused on pleasing his party's conservative base is going to defy its activists on the issue that most of them care more about than any other.

I don't like the idea of using litmus tests for judicial nominees. As a senator who must regularly vote on whether to confirm federal judges to lifetime appointments, I prefer to take a long, serious look at their qualifications and their judicial philosophy rather than try to determine how they might rule in hypothetical cases.

But I will say this. The Supreme Court hangs in the balance and the next justices will determine whether we move forward or backward. Therefore, I will filibuster any Supreme Court nominee who would turn back the clock on the right to choose, on civil rights and individual liberties, on the laws protecting workers and the environment. I believe the twenty-first century should be about progress. And if elected president, I will nominate judges who will seek to expand rights and opportunities—not reduce them. In this area, anyone who values a woman's right to choose in particular or constitutional privacy rights in general will have the clearest possible choice between me and President Bush in 2004.

From my point of view, respecting the equal rights of citizens is not simply a negative exercise in stopping discrimination or removing artificial obstacles. It's also a positive exercise in engaging Americans in the responsibilities as well as the rights of citizenship. That's why I believe that reviving democracy in our country depends on a much more active concept of citizenship. Citizenship should be more than the fact of birth or immigration status; it should answer a call to service in self-government.

As I hope I made clear in the first chapter of this book, I'm running for president in no small part because I want this country to be a place where citizens don't think of themselves as passive consumers of government services and benefits in competition with other consumers. This is an idea that both parties have unfortunately encouraged in the recent past with their competing agendas of expanded government benefits or bigger tax cuts. I want Americans to think of their country as a true commonwealth and of government as nothing more or less than an instrument for self-government.

I myself grew up as the son of a public employee. To be sure, the diplomatic service, in which my father worked for much of his adult life, seems a lot more glamorous than many forms of public employment. But it doesn't necessarily bring higher pay, and it definitely doesn't provide either stability or tenure.

I did learn from my father, however, to respect the idea of public service in a very old-fashioned way—a way that I think we need to restore as part of a cutting-edge, twenty-first-century approach to reforming government. My father, a very able man, could have made a lot of money in private business and had a stable family and community life instead of having to worry where we would be liv-

ing from year to year. But he wanted to serve his country, and he viewed public service as contributing just as much to the peace and prosperity of his fellow citizens as anything he could do in the military or in the private sector.

Without question, there are many government employees who regard their jobs as simply jobs and who chose public service as a career as a result of some personal cost-benefit analysis of pay, benefits, and job security. There are also many people working in some of the most entrepreneurial companies in America who think that way as well, just as there are teachers who lack any passion for teaching and even members of the clergy who view their profession as just a career option.

But I know from my father's experience and from my own that literally millions of public employees will respond positively and powerfully to an effort to put the "service" back into public service. I want to work with government executives and public-sector union leaders who have the vision to see how making government agencies true public enterprises can give public employees new respect and new opportunities to express their independence and creativity. To put it another way, I don't think we can issue a call to service to Americans at large without calling on those who already serve to raise their own sights and direct their efforts to the improvement of the commonwealth.

As we ask Americans to become more involved in how their government works, we should also ask them never to neglect the minimum privilege of citizenship: the right to vote. Millions of Americans don't vote because of the excessive complexity of voting procedures, the essential simple-mindedness of campaigns, and the belief that powerful private interests ultimately outweigh the public interest in most elections.

In the contested 2000 elections we saw what can happen when there are many irregularities in ballots and registration lists, lack of information about the location of polling places, apparent efforts to intimidate minority or new-citizen voting, inconsistent ways of handling absentee ballots, and, most famously, methods of counting or recounting ballots once they were cast. While Florida officials took a lot of flak for these irregularities, the high stakes of that particular outcome, in fact, cast the world's brightest spotlight on problems that exist all over the country.

The election reform legislation that we passed in Congress in 2002 was a good start toward addressing this situation, providing a bit of money and a bit of direction to states to help them begin modernizing their voting technologies and procedures. But we are still a long way from where we ought to be, when all Americans know where and how to vote, know what offices and issues they are voting on—and know, for a certainty, that their vote will count and be counted.

These issues will be part of my campaign and if I am the Democratic nominee, I will assure my party's election-day preparations and get-out-the-vote drives. I will insist that voting laws be observed and enforced and that the federal government and the Republican Party cooperate in enforcing the law and its spirit. And if I am elected president, I will launch an initiative not only to ensure the right to vote but to experiment with a variety of ideas to engage voters and expand their power to cast informed votes on the full range of public offices and propositions.

I am constantly struck by the quite rational confusion voters experience as a result of constantly changing districts, constantly changing polling places, and unexpected ballot questions. Who among us, however public spirited and knowledgeable about the issues, hasn't entered a voting booth only to discover a bond referendum, a constitutional amendment, or candidates we know nothing about? Who among us in metropolitan areas hasn't watched televised campaign ads and wondered if the candidates will be on the ballots in our district?

I think we need to test approaches that allow for better informed and more deliberative voting. In Oregon, for example, all ballots are cast by mail, and voters have time between receiving and casting their ballots to actually do some research about candidates and issues they can vote on. Turnout in Oregon has been sky-high since this system was introduced.

Beyond reforming elections, reviving full democratic participation in the central ritual of democracy requires far more fundamental changes than we have yet seen to our sick system of financing campaigns. The McCain–Feingold reforms of 2002 were a first step in this process. I honor my two friends and colleagues for their courage and persistence in building so much support for this measure that President Bush did not dare to veto it. As of this writing, the Supreme Court is still considering a variety of challenges to McCain-Feingold, and it's unclear how many of its original provisions will survive.

Even if the decision is favorable, future campaign finance reform will still have to contend with the Supreme Court's doctrine that political contributions are a form of political speech protected by the First Amendment. As long as that is settled law, I believe we should create alternatives for candidates who choose not to join the money hunt or don't have the means to finance their own campaigns. Here are a number of specific ideas for revising the campaign process whose time has come: First, we should ask television stations that enjoy private profits from publicly controlled spectrum space to give something back by providing significant free time to candidates, including candidate debates. My experience debating Governor Bill Weld in our 1996 Senate campaign convinced me that if you provide enough positive information about candidates and their views, it will far outweigh the poisonous effects of negative campaigning, which is increasing now that private interests are running so many negative ads. Second, we should also emulate the states that are introducing systems of voluntary public financing of campaigns that are aimed at stigmatizing candidates who insist on hustling for private contributions or drawing money out of their personal fortunes. Specifically, we should take another look at Al Gore's little-discussed proposal of 2000 for a national fund that would be used to provide campaign money for congressional candidates who agree to limit private contributions and accept spending limits.

*

In 2000, George W. Bush broke, indeed obliterated, every previous record by raising and spending one hundred million dollars to secure the Republican nomination for president. He didn't even think about accepting public financing and its spending limits.

In 2004, even though he's running unopposed for the GOP nomination, he's planning to raise and spend $250 million before the Republican Convention. That's wrong—and not just for me or other Democrats, who for the sake of our beliefs would prefer at least a nearly level playing field. It's wrong for the country. Americans should be concerned about the expectations of private gain that must accompany a quarter of a billion dollars in contributions to a candidate for public office. What wilderness preserve will George W. Bush hand to the oil companies in a second term?

The president signed McCain-Feingold under duress, and if he has any concern about the corrupting effect of private money on public offices, he's kept it to himself. I will challenge him to discuss this subject, not because I expect to change his mind but because I want him to face the voters and tell them why he won't even respect the minimal campaign reforms now written into law.

Engaging Americans in all these aspects of self-government is something I'm passionate about. I'm also realistic. It's a quiet revolution and one that will take time, and as president I will definitely take the time to push the process along as fast as I can.

There's one step we can take right away, both to revive the spirit of citizenship and honor the mutual obligations between a free society and its people: give every American who is willing to perform national service the immediate opportunity to do so.

President Bush has done something worse than merely failing to hear this call to service. He himself trumpeted it, then failed to follow through. After 9/11, voluntarism soared throughout the country. Americans searched, even begged, for ways to give something back. But President Bush turned aside proposal after proposal to tap into this new and deeply patriotic spirit. When the Republican John McCain and the Democrat Evan Bayh offered a bipartisan initiative to expand national service opportunities, the president rejected it and let his closest allies in Congress bury it. He made his own call to service in his 2002 State of the Union Address, promising to greatly expand the Peace Corps and AmeriCorps. But he made no effort nor did he expend an ounce of political capital to make it happen. He promised to rally "the armies of compassion" then put aside his bugle and left them high and dry at the first sign of right-wing opposition.

To me, the issue is clear. When Americans want to serve, we should help them. It can't possibly cost more than alternative, government-oriented ways to deal with big social problems, like poor kids who need mentors or reading tutors, crime-ridden neighborhoods that need patrols, or simply volunteers eager to give their time who need someone to organize and deploy them.

We have seen throughout our history what happens when we appeal to the best instincts of Americans. Franklin D. Roosevelt summoned his fellow citizens to stand tall against the tide of the Great Depression. Seventy years ago, his Civilian Conservation Corps sent millions of the young out to rebuild the nation even as they built a better life for themselves. John Kennedy called my generation to the Peace Corps, and Lyndon Johnson's VISTA opened up the chance to serve in the most forgotten places in our own land, including the inner city, Appalachia, and Native American reservations. Only ten years ago President Clinton introduced AmeriCorps and inaugurated a new generation of service.

I propose building on that tradition and also going beyond it, because today our challenges are different and our commitment must be even greater. We need a new era of service—not merely an effort for a single occasion, a single purpose, or a single group but a permanent national endeavor to make service an obligation of citizenship.

To do that, we need a seamless web of service in which every American—young and old, rich and poor, of every race, religion, and background—can enlist in a new army of patriots who will serve on all the frontlines of our future. These include guarding our nation from danger abroad, strengthening our homeland security, reducing illiteracy, preserving our environment, providing after-school care, helping our seniors live in dignity, building new homes for those who need them—and through all these activities, building a nation that is more truly one America.

My proposal is to engage more than a million Americans a year in voluntary full- or part-time national service positions, with millions more volunteering some portion of their time and talents in less formal ways.

A new Service for College initiative will call on young people both to reinforce America's security and to address unmet needs. For every young person who gives two years of service, America will pay the cost for four years of his or her public college tuition. This will simultaneously strengthen our society, enhance our economy, and advance our values by opening doors of higher education to those who respond to a higher sense of duty.

We have a good foundation in place in AmeriCorps, which in the past ten years has gone from a good idea to a great success. Thousands of young people have served in inner-city and rural schools, built low-income housing, and rebuilt communities after natural disasters. State and local initiative has led the way; the bureaucracy in Washington, which has been held to a minimum, has stepped to the side.

But in this administration, AmeriCorps has been cut and capped. I believe that this is wrong—in terms of both our national work and our national spirit. As president, I will bring national service out of the shadows and into the center of national purpose.

My aim is nothing less than to make national service a way of life for each new generation of Americans. To that end, I will set a goal within the next decade of enlisting five hundred thousand young people a year in Service for College—more than one out of seven young Americans working side by side, in many different pursuits, with a common commitment to our best hopes and values.

Just think of what a force of this size and dedication can accomplish. AmeriCorps members already are playing a part in providing homeland security. All around the country, they have participated in emergency drills. They have helped the Red Cross to conduct disaster-preparedness training and mobilized local communities to assemble emergency-response plans. With even a greater number in service we can do far more to safeguard this country. This is the time for young people to step forward with patriotism and pride and volunteer to prepare America for and protect it from the threats we face.

Helping our communities become prepared to prevent or meet terrorist acts requires more than thousands of officials sitting in a new agency in Washington. It will take thousands of trained people on the ground ready to work with firefighters, police officers, health professionals, and other first defenders to protect our communities and react if an attack does come. Service members can participate in coordinating efforts in hospitals, searching for vulnerabilities at our ports, and enlisting local volunteers and showing them how to do their part.

America's young are more than equal to this great responsibility. It was young people who stormed the beaches and climbed the cliffs of Normandy and raised the flag over Iwo Jima. Many of the police and firefighters who ran up the stairs of the World Trade Center were young. It was primarily the young who put their lives on the line in Afghanistan and Iraq.

But this is the beginning not the end of the difference their service can make, for they can change the face of American life. With their help, more senior citizens will be able to live independently in their own homes instead of in nursing homes. With their help, we can achieve a national goal of having every child reading by the third grade. They can assist teachers, parents, and administrators in making sure that our schools are once again the best in the world. With their help, we'll start our youngest children on the path to success by making sure they have the care and support they need in the critical early years of their development. And with their help, we'll make the hardest job in the world—being a parent—a little easier by giving moms and dads more support in the uphill struggle to balance work and family. Those who serve will work in summer and after-school programs where more American children can learn in safety and grow up as strong citizens. Servers will battle soil erosion in our rural areas, bring new life to urban parks in our cities, and join with groups like YouthBuild and Habitat for Humanity to build affordable housing in America's neighborhoods.

Service members are not professionals. Nothing can ever replace a skilled firefighter, teacher, nurse, child-care provider, or conservation engineer who does a critical job with professionalism and pride. But everyone and every task can use a helping hand—and we can do more for America if young Americans give more of themselves.

America has already seen the impact of enlisting the young in meeting some of our hardest challenges. For nearly ten years, young people have received partial assistance in paying for college in exchange for a commitment to serve as police officers after graduation. The Police Corps is an idea I've championed from the start; it has been one of the most innovative initiatives of the last decade. As president, I will expand it so that it will continue to provide an even higher level of benefits covering all four years of college. Whether the young people who are members of the corps stay in police work or serve and go on to other careers, they make our streets safer while they are in uniform and, in a larger sense, whether in uniform or afterward, they will strengthen our rule of law and our shared understanding of rights and responsibilities.

No lesson our students can learn is more important than citizenship. Teaching them about the rights and responsibilities they have as Americans is as vital as teaching them algebra or literature. Literacy about democracy is the lifeblood of a free society. Yet in a recent national test, more than 45 percent of twelfth graders couldn't explain how democracy benefits from citizen participation. That's our failing, not theirs. We need to teach democratic values in our classrooms and educate students not only about how a bill becomes a law but about how they can become fully participating citizens.

Because they should live as well as learn those lessons,

I propose that all high school students be required to perform community service before they graduate. Today, the State of Maryland, many school districts around the country, and many individual high schools already require service. They have proven its worth and shown that it is not mere make-work but something that can make a difference in many lives and enrich all our communities. Communities can design these efforts to meet their own specific needs, whether it be providing after-school activities for younger kids, tutoring them in reading, spending time with seniors, or helping to clean up and renew neighborhoods. There is a world of work for students to do and a nation of extraordinary volunteer organizations ready and eager to recruit them.

States and local communities will design their own service requirements to make the commitment significant without being onerous. For instance, Maryland's requirement is seventy-five hours over the course of high school. Local educators have the discretion to implement this in ways that meet student needs. Nothing in this plan will prevent young people who need to earn money for college from doing so. Certainly fifty to a hundred hours in the four years of high school doesn't seem too much to ask from young people as they take on the responsibility of being a citizen. We can and will assist local communities in shaping high school service plans to fit what they seek to accomplish—and then we must assure them sufficient resources to put those plans in place.

While high school service should be mandatory for

students, it must not become another unfunded mandate from Washington. I propose that unless the federal government fully funds this service requirement, states will not have to implement it. Government needs to do more than teach the next generation responsibility; it needs to show some of its own. If Washington doesn't do its part, young people won't be required to do theirs.

And there is something else they can do if we give them the chance. Teenagers thirteen to seventeen are too old for child care and too young for many summer jobs. Parents don't want to leave them alone all summer, but many families don't have any alternative. I propose summers of service, a program that will involve teenagers in the work of their communities. Supervised by AmeriCorps volunteers, they can visit nursing homes, clean up local areas, or teach seniors computer skills. In turn, they will earn a grant to apply to their college tuition.

Next, I propose service not by the young in years but by those who still have much to contribute after finishing their careers. As Robert Kennedy once said: "Youth is not a time of life but a state of mind." As president, I will defend and strengthen fundamental guarantees, such as Social Security and Medicare. I also believe in calling on retired Americans to contribute to a nation that continues to need all that they have to offer, which is the basis for my proposal for older Americans in service. Today's Americans are living longer and staying healthier well into their retirement; we need their experience and their energy. In return, they will earn money that they can apply to an education grant for a grandchild or any other child they choose.

These men and women have already done so much for their country. They can now do likewise for their communities: Older Americans can serve as positive role models for our children, signposts of stability in our classrooms, and the world's most patient tutors. When they become part of schools, students behave better. When older Americans spend time tutoring, children learn more and learn faster. And older Americans have the credibility and compassion to help their own infirm or disabled peers in ways that no one else can. Our older Americans are retired, not tired, and America cannot afford to waste their wisdom and vitality.

In another, very specific way, more Americans can do something vital for the nation through a new community defense service of hundreds of thousands of people in thousands of local areas. Like crime watches in many of our neighborhoods, community defense service captains will help show Americans how they and their families can best prepare for the threats we face. These volunteers will provide their neighbors with solid, reliable information about biological, chemical, and other terrorist threats. Ameri-Corps members will organize the effort, the Department of Homeland Security will offer leadership, and firefighters and police officers will furnish the necessary training and education. The members of the community defense service will be there working side by side with first defenders whenever and wherever they are needed.

In any proposal for national service, attention must be paid to the Peace Corps, the most powerful and respected symbol of nonmilitary service in our history. If there was ever a time when people in the most deprived countries, cities, and villages of the world need to see idealistic Americans working to help them, it is today in the aftermath of September 11. Peace Corps members are the greatest ambassadors of goodwill and democracy this nation has ever had—and we need more of them. Today, there are sixty-seven hundred Peace Corps volunteers, far fewer than in the 1960s, even when much of the globe was off-limits during the cold war. I propose a major expansion of the Peace Corps for this new century to twenty-five thousand members. They will serve in the places they always have as well as in new areas of challenge—the Middle East and communities in Africa ravaged by AIDS. The Peace Corps will once again be treated as one of America's proudest and most important endeavors.

Finally, there is military service, which has made and kept this country free, defended it from mortal dangers, and saved the world from the most monstrous forms of tyranny. The military is an honorable and noble calling and so often the highest form of sacrifice. As president, I will seek to strengthen our armed forces by providing more resources and better inducements to recruit more active-duty personnel. The difficult missions we face and the complex technologies we depend on demand that. And when so many reservists are also firefighters and police officers, relying exclusively on activating them at a time of crisis can actually weaken our security. President Bush has not led in recruit-ing young people into the military. I will. And as president, I will modernize our GI Bill benefits. Those who risk their lives for America deserve the best chance for an excellent education and to earn a better life for their families.

☆

I learned about duty and obligation from my parents—through their words and by their example. I described ear-lier in this chapter my mother's lifelong community work as an environmental activist. My father set aside his career and volunteered even before America entered World War II. While he was away on duty, my mother sent him a letter saying, "You have no idea of the ways in which one can be useful right now. There's something for everyone to do."

Two decades later, Martin Luther King told us: "Everybody can be great because everybody can serve." To-day America will be secure and strong if everybody does serve, because there is work for all to do, a place for all to serve, and no reason to stay on the sidelines.

I see an America where citizens of all ages and back-grounds can make a difference and meet an obligation higher than themselves.

I see an America where, in a seamless web of service and concern, we offer Americans the challenge and the chance to do their duty—and an America where Ameri-cans, in turn, step forward and give something back.

I see an America where in times of trouble and triumph, of threat and hope, we ask not just what government can do, but what we can do, as President Kennedy so memorably suggested.

That's why I'm running for president, and that's why I have organized my campaign agenda around a call to service.

It was my generation that in its youth heard that call. We did not think we were special; we simply believed in doing our part. And in the end, I suppose that is all any of us can do, and I believe each of us must try.

Our great country, the world's oldest and strongest democracy, can become even greater if we commit ourselves to helping one another here at home and helping others beyond our borders achieve the values of freedom and democracy that we have championed to the envy of the whole world.

This is my call to service and yours.

Acknowledgments

Producing a substantive book in the midst of performing the duties of a senator, not to mention running for president, is obviously a task in which I relied on the generous help of many talented and trusted associates.

Thanks first to Ed Kilgore, whose broad policy knowledge and understanding of my record and agenda helped me organize my thoughts and ensure a coherent and consistent text.

I also want to thank my Senate chief of staff, David McKean, who supervised the project from beginning to end and made sure I met my deadlines.

Rick Kot and Adrian Zackheim of Viking Penguin were editors who understood the pressures and distractions I was working under and made the production of this book a smooth and relatively painless experience.

I want to thank a number of people who read the manuscript at various stages and who made useful comments and suggestions. They include, from my presidential campaign team, David Wade, Jim Jordan, Bob Shrum, Sarah Bianchi, Heather Higginbottom, and Mike Gehrke. George Abar and Dr. Nancy Stetson of my Senate staff also volunteered some of their own time to help. My good and wise friends Dr. David Hamburg and Eric Hamburg offered suggestions as well, as did Jeff Lewis of the Heinz Family Foundations.

As always, my wife, Teresa, provided advice and support, along with the example she constantly sets in the policy work she undertakes at the Heinz Family Foundations.

These people share my personal "call to service," and I am proud they have shared the stimulating if sometimes heavy burden of articulating an agenda to answer that call in 2004 and beyond.